The New York Times

Guide to
Economics

Cheryl D. Jennings, Ph.D.
Gus A. Stavros Center for Free
Enterprise & Economic Education
Florida State University

Bernard F. Sliger, Ph.D.
Gus A. Stavros Center for Free
Enterprise & Economic Education
Florida State University

Jamie Murphy, Ph.D.
Visiting Fellow, Department of Information
Management and Marketing
University of Western Australia

 South-Western College Publishing
Thomson Learning™

Australia • Canada • Denmark • Japan • Mexico • New Zealand • Philippines
Puerto Rico • Singapore • South Africa • Spain • United Kingdom • United States

The New York Times Guide to Economics, by Cheryl D. Jennings & Bernard F. Sliger

Publisher: Dave Shaut
Acquisitions Editor: Pamela M. Person
Marketing Manager: Rob Bloom
Production Editor: Elizabeth A. Shipp
Media and Technology Editor: Kevin von Gillern
Media Production Editor: Robin K. Browning
Manufacturing Coordinator: Sandee Milewski
Internal Design: Joe Devine
Cover Design: Joe Devine
Copyeditor: Brian L. Massey
Production House: Trejo Production
Printer: Webcom

Printed in Canada
1 2 3 4 5 03 02 01 00

For more information contact South-Western College Publishing, 5101 Madison Road, Cincinnati, Ohio, 45227 or find us on the Internet at http://www.swcollege.com

For permission to use material from this text or product, contact us by
• **telephone: 1-800-730-2214**
• **fax: 1-800-730-2215**
• **web: http://www.thomsonrights.com**

Library of Congress Cataloging-in-Publication Data
Jennings, Cheryl D., 1954–
     The New York Times guide to economics / Cheryl D. Jennings, Bernard F.
Sliger, Jamie Murphy.
     p. cm.
     ISBN 0-324-04159-4 (alk. paper)
        1. Economics.   I. Title: Guide to economics.   II. Sliger, Bernard F.   III. Murphy,
Jamie, 1950–   IV. New York Times.   V. Title.

HB71.J46   2000
330--dc21   00-021220

This book is printed on acid-free paper.

P R E F A C E

....

The New York Times Guide to Economics is designed for students, professors and business professionals—anyone interested in staying current in business today. A collection of the best economics-related articles from the *New York Times*, this guide does more than inform: it also provides context for the effects of change on all aspects of business. Also included are articles from *CyberTimes*, the online-only technology section of the *New York Times on the Web*. Each article was selected for its relevance to today's business world.

In purchasing *The New York Times Guide to Economics,* you are not only purchasing the contents between the covers, but also unlimited access, via password, to related *New York Times* articles. Current articles will be linked from the South-Western College Publishing/*New York Times* Web site (http://nytimes.swcollege.com) on an ongoing basis as news breaks.

This guide can be used formally in the classroom or informally for life-long learning. All articles are accompanied by exploratory exercises and probing questions developed by experts in the field. Previews provide context for each chapter of articles and link them to key economic principles. This guide is divided into six sections organized to highlight critical factors in economics today. This organization allows for easy integration into any economics course.

Chapter 1: Fundamentals of Economics. This opening chapter focuses on the most fundamental problem in economics—scarcity. Topics include: economic definitions, scarcity, choice, specialization, economic reasoning, rational decision-making, laws of supply and demand, economic theories, economic principles, economic models and economic systems.

Chapter 2: Macroeconomics. This chapter explores the large dimensions of economic activity and the institutions that attempt to regulate these activities. Topics include: money and banking, fiscal policy, government taxing and spending, monetary policy, the Federal Reserve, financial institutions, unemployment, inflation, the Federal budget, public debt, the business cycle and economic measures.

Chapter 3: Microeconomics. This chapter focuses on the "micro" or small elements of the economy. Topics include: market models (e.g., pure competition, monopoly), business structures and organization, labor markets, public finance, public choice, consumer choice and demand, consumer prices and antitrust (e.g., price-fixing, mergers).

Chapter 4: Personal Economics. Intelligent consumers are knowledgeable about their personal finances, but are likewise well aware of the overall "consumer health" of the economy. Topics include: savings, investing, credit, insurance and retirement.

Chapter 5: Global Economics. Globalization is rapidly altering the economic landscape at home and abroad. Topics include: foreign exchange markets, international monetary systems, trade barriers, global competition, global trade and specialization.

Chapter 6: Other Economic Issues. This chapter focuses on the future, especially the impact of technology. Topics include: technology, the information age, new communication technologies, economic forecasting, environmental economics and careers in economics.

PEDAGOGICAL FEATURES

Critical Thinking Questions challenge you to form your own opinion about current topics. These questions can be used to stimulate classroom discussion or as the basis for formal assignments.

Story-specific Questions highlight important points from each story.

Short Application Assignments work well as hands-on exercises for both classroom discussion and formal assignments. Most assignments should take no more than a few hours to complete. Typical assignments include developing presentations and writing brief memos, reports, executive summaries and articles for company newsletters.

Building Research Skills exercises allow you to expand upon what you have learned from the *New York Times'* articles and explore the unlimited resources available to enhance your understanding of current events. Typical assignments include presentations, writing essays and building Web pages.

ADDITIONAL ONLINE PEDAGOGY

Sample Exercises provide examples for you to follow in completing assignments.

Additional Readings link to more than 100 additional stories, categorized by chapter, for further research.

Featured Sections are in-depth collections of stories on specific topics such as Social Security, Outlook 2000, The World Financial Crisis, Russia in Turmoil, Asia's Financial Crisis, The Euro and the New Europe, The Federal Reserve,

Retirement, the U.S. Budget, Welfare, Looking Back at the Crash of '29 and Is Microsoft a Monopoly.

Book Reviews cover about 80 computer and digital technology books reviewed by the *New York Times*, listed alphabetically by author and linked to the original review.

ACKNOWLEDGMENTS

I am deeply indebted to many individuals who generously contributed to this publication. Among these are Dr. Bernard F. Sliger, Florida State University President Emeritus and Director of the Gus A. Stavros Center for Free Enterprise & Economic Education. Dr. Sliger, a well-known economist, provided expert suggestions for each chapter. Additionally, I sincerely appreciate Jamie Murphy, who patiently guided me through this project. He cheerfully gave me valuable feedback, content recommendations, and encouragement when I needed it most. I certainly could not have completed this publication without Jamie's help. I also thank Dr. Brian L. Massey, Nanyang Technological University, Singapore, who kindly contributed insightful editing suggestions that helped the text come alive.

Finally, I want to thank Larry Jennings, my husband and friend, who would not allow me to give up on preparing this publication. As always, his kind and gentle spirit prevailed during the most difficult phases of the project. I am forever grateful for his support.

C O N T E N T S

CHAPTER 1
Fundamentals of Economics **1**

Bills Reopen Debate Over Visa Limit 2
Jeri Clausing

Debate Over Visas for Foreign Workers Focuses on Layoffs 6
Jeri Clausing

It's Raining Farm Subsidies 10
Tim Weiner

CHAPTER 2
Macroeconomics **15**

Focus Shifts to the Central Bank's Long-Term Agenda 16
Richard W. Stevenson

Central Bank Raises Interest Rates to Avert Inflation 21
Richard W. Stevenson

Inflation Just Doesn't Add Up 25
Sylvia Nasar

CHAPTER 3
Microeconomics **31**

Antitrust in the Slow Lane 33
Steve Lohr

U.S. Judge Declares Microsoft a Monopoly That Stifles Industry 36
Joel Brinkley

As Welfare Benefits Expire, Second Thoughts 41
Jason DeParle

CHAPTER 4
Personal Economics   **49**

Gap Between Rich and Poor Found Substantially Wider   50
David Cay Johnston

A Growing Gap Between the Savers and the Save-Nots   54
David Cay Johnston

Great Expectations: The Retirement Mentality vs. Reality   59
Barbara Crosette

CHAPTER 5
Global Economics   **63**

Crash Course: Just What's Driving the Crisis in Emerging Markets?   65
Louis Uchitelle

U.S. Reaches an Accord to Open China Economy as Worldwide Market   70
Erik Eckholm with David E. Sanger

A Deal the United States Just Couldn't Refuse   76
David E. Sanger

China Sets Up Its Own Web Site to Lure U.S. Concerns' Business   80
Bob Tedeschi

CHAPTER 6
Other Economics Issues   **83**

Productivity as the Catalyst of Prosperity   85
Deborah Stead

Computer Age Gains Respect of Economists   88
Steve Lohr

Debate on Internet Taxes Takes Political Turn   94
Jeri Clausing

Internet Tax Panel Faces Thorny Issues   97
Jeri Clausing

CHAPTER 1

Fundamentals of Economics

PREVIEW

Solving problems of scarcity is perhaps the most important purpose of economics. Scarcity exists, to some degree, in every society. The ways to resolve scarcity vary, however, and depend upon the economic limitations or strengths within a nation's economy. When economic policy decisions are made, concern about scarcity usually drives them. Economists address the phenomenon of scarcity by formulating theories, principles and laws to explain or solve it.

For example, some people argue that there is a "shortage" of skilled workers in the American workforce. Economists would address this scarcity by considering the perceived need to fill job vacancies with workers who would be the most capable at increasing productivity. Because of this workforce scarcity, the debate over allowing highly educated immigrants to enter the United States has intensified recently.

Source: Christine M. Thompson/CyberTimes

Jeri Clausing revs up the workforce-scarcity discussion in her article "Bills Reopen Debate Over Visa Limit," in which she examines recent legislation to allow more skilled foreign workers to enter the United States. Her complementary article, "Debate Over Visas for Foreign Workers Focuses on Layoffs," discusses competition between American and foreign workers.

Subsidies, with which the government helps someone pay for something, are another solution for scarcity. But as Tim Weiner illustrates in "It's Raining Farm Subsidies," federal farm policy seems to create bigger farms and less farmers. Critics say that America's farm subsidies bring "precious little benefit—and, some argue, great harm—to small farmers trying to make a living."

Bills Reopen Debate Over Visa Limit

By Jeri Clausing

Washington—Just one year after the high-tech industry won a tough political fight to hire more skilled foreign workers, Republican leaders are re-igniting the contentious debate that some say underscores the need for more permanent immigration reforms.

The Clinton Administration remains opposed to any further increase in temporary visas for educated workers, saying the industry needs to focus on training people domestically to meet its employment needs. But no one is dismissing the chance that new legislation to raise the number of so-called H1-B visas could pass after Congress returns from a monthlong recess next week, particularly as Republicans and Democrats compete to be seen as the party most friendly to the high-tech industry.

Just before Congress headed out for its August break, three bills were filed to allow companies to hire more foreign workers on temporary visas. Proposals by Senator Phil Gramm, a Texas Republican, and Representative David Dreier, a California Republican, would nearly double the number of H1-B visas reserved for skilled workers, to 200,000 from 115,000.

Additionally, Representative Zoe Lofgren, a Democrat who represents California's Silicon Valley, has filed a bill that would create a new class of visas for foreign students with science degrees, which would be in addition to the H1-B visas high-tech companies now rely on.

Meanwhile, Senator John McCain, an Arizona Republican who is running for President, said he intends to file another bill in September that would increase the visa cap to 175,000 a year and give the U.S. Labor Secretary the authority to raise the limit beyond that if necessary.

Those proposals come just a year after Congress raised the cap on H1-Bs from 65,000—despite accusations that companies were using the visas to hire cheap, young foreign workers to replace more experienced Americans who have been hit by layoffs.

High-tech companies and major trade groups like the Information Technology Association of America said they would welcome any and all of the bills, but they have so far declined to enter the debate on Capitol Hill.

Five companies turned down invitations to testify at a hearing of the House Immigration Subcommittee just before the Congress's summer break. Those close to the process say high-tech companies are waiting and watching, because they are hesitant to reenter what turned into one of the industry's toughest political battles last year, and because they have been focusing this year on several other key items. Leading the industry's agenda are efforts to pass legislation limiting high-tech companies' liability in the event of Year 2000 equipment failures and winning a permanent extension of a tax credit for research and development.

Renee Winsky, a vice president of the ITAA, said she was unsure what prompted the new round of proposals, which began with an announcement earlier this summer by Gramm during a visit to Texas Instruments. She said none of her members have even called to suggest that the ITAA push the issue.

Although she contends more visas are needed, Winsky said that for now, she is working to develop longer-term solutions for what the industry says is a critical worker shortage.

"Certainly, we are not going to come out in opposition to something that helps our members' companies," Winsky said. "But everyone knows that long-term, we have to look at employment immigration. We have a skills gap, we have a gap in our workforce that's not going to be fixed by just increasing the visas for three years."

"This is something that's not going to go away with last year's increase or anything that is going to pass this year."

The proposals come just a year after Congress approved increasing the cap on H1-Bs to 115,000 from 65,000 after a tough battle with the White House that finally resulted in a compromise that added an application fee for the H1-B visas to finance domestic training programs. But because that battle dragged on for months longer than anticipated, it created a backlog of visa applications from 1998 that resulted in this year's cap being hit early as well. Likewise, officials fear that the backlog of applications now piling up will mean that next year's limit will also be reached early.

But with the new bills comes a renewed debate over whether there really is a critical shortage of skilled Americans capable of filling openings in the fast-growing information technology sector, or whether the companies are just trying to keep wages down.

To address questions about wages, last year's bill called for better record keeping on the salaries being paid H1-B recipients, but the new procedures are not yet in place. That means no federal agency yet has an accurate count of how much H1-B workers are being paid. And studies from the Department of Commerce and Department of Labor have been unable to prove conclusively that there is a high-tech labor shortage.

Additionally, testimony at House Immigration Subcommittee hearings this year have raised questions about whether the INS count of the visas is accurate. There are also indications that fraud is a serious problem in the program, according to the subcommittee's chairman, Representative Lamar Smith, a Texas Republican.

At the hearing, witnesses from the Immigration and Naturalization Service and the State Department described a spot check of 3,247 H1-B petitions issued by the consulate in Chennai, India.

"The results were staggering—45 percent of the cases could not be authenticated and 21 percent were identified as outright fraudulent," Smith wrote to Doris Meissner, the INS Commissioner. "Chennai issued more than 15,000 H1-B visas in fiscal year 1998. A significant portion of those visas may have been issued on the basis of fraudulent or unverifiable documentation."

"Non-government witnesses who testified at the May hearing, including a representative of large corporations that rely on the H1-B program to obtain key personnel and two immigration attorneys, agreed that fraud is a serous problem in the H1-B program," the letter said. "They expressed concern that the large number of fraudulent petitions severely reduces the number of visas available to legitimate employers."

Smith asked Meissner to take steps to crack down on fraud, but she has not yet responded to the letter. An INS official said a response would be sent within 60 days.

Allen Kay, a spokesman for Smith, said the congressmen will be looking closely at all the bills when Congress returns in September. But he said that Smith, like Winsky, would like to focus any new debate on longer-term reforms of the system for permanent immigrants rather than temporary visa programs.

CyberTimes, The New York Times on the Web, August 31, 1999
http://www.nytimes.com/library/tech/99/08/cyber/capital/31capital.html

CRITICAL THINKING QUESTIONS

1. Labor unions serve as a vehicle for expressing the concerns of employees. Explain your position on labor union involvement in the regulation of visas issued by the government.
2. Should a company be obliged to hire laid-off workers before hiring at a lower wage young, foreign employees with visas? Why, or why not?
3. What effect do you think our aging population, which is staying in the workforce longer, will have on immigration policies in the future?

STORY-SPECIFIC QUESTIONS

1. What does the Clinton Administration recommend as a remedy to the current U.S. worker shortage?
2. How much of an increase is recommended in the number of visas issued over the last year?
3. What advantages will high-tech companies have if more visas are issued?

SHORT APPLICATION ASSIGNMENTS

1. In teams or individually, answer the story-specific questions; keep your answers to 25–75 words for each question.

2. In teams of three to five persons each, or as a whole class, discuss your responses to the critical thinking questions.
3. Prepare a one-page memo report (200–250 words) to your instructor in which you summarize this article. You will find a model one-page report on the Web site (nytimes.swcollege.com).
4. Write an executive summary (200–250 words). As an administrative assistant to a busy executive, you are expected to summarize selected articles and present important points. You will find a model executive summary on the Web site.
5. Summarize this article (100–125 words) for your company's newsletter. You will find a model newsletter on the Web site.

BUILDING RESEARCH SKILLS

1. Individually or in teams, investigate the status of current labor shortages in the United States. In what area is there the most critical need? Your instructor may ask you to submit a three- to five-page essay, post a Web page or report your results in a five-minute presentation, along with a letter of transmittal explaining your essay.
2. Individually or in teams, investigate anticipated labor shortages in the United States for the next five to 10 years. Develop a proposal detailing measures you would recommend in order to avoid a "labor scarcity" problem in the future. Your instructor may ask you to submit a three- to five-page proposal, post a Web page or report your results in a five-minute presentation, along with a letter of transmittal explaining your proposal.
3. Using at least three other references (e.g., books, research-journal articles, newspaper or magazine stories or credible Web sites), write an 800- to 1,000-word essay that addresses two of the critical thinking questions offered earlier. Assume that your essay will be used as an internal reference for a government's policy guidelines.
4. Using at least three other references (e.g., books, research-journal articles, newspaper or magazine stories or credible Web sites), post an 800- to 1,000-word Web page that addresses at least two of the earlier critical thinking questions. Assume that your page will be posted in the policy section of a government's intranet.

Debate Over Visas for Foreign Workers Focuses on Layoffs

By Jeri Clausing

Washington—Prominent companies who hire large numbers of engineers and other high-tech workers have laid off more Americans in the past six months than the number of temporary foreign workers that information technology companies are lobbying to bring in over the next three years, U.S. Representative Lamar Smith said Tuesday.

Between December, 1997 and June, 1998, 21 well-known high-tech companies dismissed 121,800 workers, according to figures compiled by the Chicago-based employment firm Challenger, Grey and Christmas.

During the same period, the information technology industry launched an aggressive lobbying campaign to increase the number of so-called H1-B visas for skilled temporary foreign workers by 120,000 through 2001. Technology companies say they need to import more workers because of a shortage of technically proficient domestic workers able to fill crucial electrical engineering and product development jobs.

Although Smith is sponsoring one of the bills that would increase the number of H1-B visas, he is at odds with the high-tech industry over provisions in his bill that would require companies using the visas to certify that Americans are not being laid off and replaced with cheaper foreign labor.

Those provisions are backed by the Clinton Administration. But the Senate rejected attempts to add such protections last month when it passed a bill by Senator Spencer Abraham, a Michigan Republican, to raise the H1-B cap.

The current annual limit of 65,000 H1-B visas was reached in May, four months shy of the end of the fiscal year. And the deadlock over the layoff provision threatens to prevent final passage of any legislation in time to provide any immediate relief for high-tech companies.

Smith, a Texas Republican who chairs the House Immigration Subcommittee, said on Tuesday that House leaders have said they would like him to reach a compromise with Abraham before they will bring his bill to a full House vote. Smith said he has placed several calls to Abraham's office but has not yet received a response.

Despite the critical labor shortage the companies say they face, business groups lobbying for the Abraham bill said they would rather have no legislation than see the Smith bill passed.

"The House bill creates more government red tape that essentially renders the whole H1-B program useless," said Bruce Josten, the executive vice president of government affairs for the U.S. Chamber of Commerce. "We need to expand the pool of highly trained foreign workers immediately, without government micromanagement, if we want American business to remain number one globally."

Josten made the comments at a news conference Tuesday where business representatives and H1-B workers who are faced with losing their work status called for quick passage of the Abraham bill.

"The moratorium on hiring highly skilled foreign professionals exacerbates what is already one of the most significant skilled worker shortages our country has experienced," said Jerry Jasinowski of the National Association of Manufacturers.

"The House is adding insult to injury by weighing down a simple cap increase with unnecessary government intrusion. If the House had adopted the Senate language, U.S. employers would now have access to a small but necessary number of temporary skilled workers."

Asked about the layoff numbers released by Smith, Josten said he didn't have specific information on those particular layoffs, but that he suspects most do not involve the highly skilled programmers and product developers companies like Intel and Microsoft say they have the most difficult time recruiting.

Intel, which has been at the forefront of the lobbying effort to increase the H1-B visa cap, challenged the numbers released by Smith. Bill Calder, a company spokesman, said the company has not been handing out pink slips but that it has "redeployed" some of its workforce, meaning employees are given four months to find new jobs in the company.

Calder also emphasized that the company uses the visas for very select, high-level product development and programming jobs, which are always difficult to fill, even when production line jobs and other positions are getting cut.

"These are highly skilled, highly educated workers . . . and there simply are not enough of them for the jobs that are available," Calder said.

Josten said he suspects that many of the layoffs are related to the downturn in the Asian economy, and therefore affect a different set of workers.

"I would suspect that is the Asian contagion rearing its ugly head," Josten said. "What I don't know is, are some of those layoffs tied to flexible scheduling of shifts in the manufacturing process, as opposed to the high-tech development side of the process."

Also on Smith's list were companies like AT&T and Kodak, which have been undergoing major restructuring, Josten pointed out.

At the news conference, H1-B workers from TRW Inc. and Texas Instruments described how they face the loss of their jobs despite vacancies at their companies because the current annual cap of 65,000 visas was reached in early May.

Valentina Videva, a manufacturing engineer for Texas Instruments who earned her degree in mechanical engineering in the United States, was just finishing her practical training at TI when the cap on H1-B visas was reached.

"As a manufacturing engineer for Texas Instruments, I was responsible for making sure our machinery ran smoothly. When that equipment malfunctions, TI stands to lose $500 a minute or more. Forty people counted on me to keep the machinery running; their jobs depended on it. Now I don't know what I should do: Should I return to Macedonia? Or will the H1-B cap be increased so I can stay here?"

Despite the layoff numbers, Smith reiterated his support for increasing the number of temporary foreign workers because "advances in computer technology have been important to America's economic growth."

But in a press release that accompanied the list of high-tech companies that have laid off workers over the past six months he asked, "What is so wrong with asking companies to advertise jobs and hire qualified American workers first?"

"Where have those 122,000 American workers gone after losing their jobs?" asked Smith. "Have U.S. firms recruited those Americans as actively as they have sought foreign workers?"

CyberTimes, The New York Times on the Web, June 17, 1998
http://www.nytimes.com/library/tech/98/06/cyber/articles/17visa.html

CRITICAL THINKING QUESTIONS

1. Should the government regulate how many people enter the United States on visas annually? Why, or why not?
2. Why should U.S. corporations be concerned about a labor shortage in the United States when so many people in this country are still unemployed?
3. Is importing workers a prudent means of eliminating a labor shortage? Why, or why not?

STORY-SPECIFIC QUESTIONS

1. On what grounds are high-tech companies laying off American workers?
2. What does Lamar Smith include as a provision to his proposal for increasing the number of visas?
3. How has Intel dealt with the issue of filling highly-skilled positions in its company?

SHORT APPLICATION ASSIGNMENTS

1. In teams or individually, answer the story-specific questions; keep your answers to 25–75 words for each question.
2. In teams of three to five persons each, or as a whole class, discuss your responses to the critical thinking questions.
3. Prepare a one-page memo report (200–250 words) to your instructor in which you summarize this article. You will find a model one-page report on the Web site (nytimes.swcollege.com).

4. Write an executive summary (200–250 words). As an administrative assistant to a busy executive, you are expected to summarize selected articles and present important points. You will find a model executive summary on the Web site.
5. Summarize this article (100–125 words) for your company's newsletter. You will find a model newsletter on the Web site.

BUILDING RESEARCH SKILLS

1. Individually or in teams, explore various Internet web sites to research labor trends. From where are most foreign workers coming? What skills do they have? In what occupational settings are they placed in the United States? What effect do you think this pool of workers has on the nation's productivity? Your instructor may ask you to submit a three- to five-page essay, post a Web page or report your results in a five-minute presentation, along with a letter of transmittal explaining your essay.
2. Individually or in teams, review several other *New York Times* articles on visas for foreign workers. Your instructor may ask you to submit a three- to five-page summary or post a Web page, along with a letter of transmittal explaining the project. As you develop your essay, reconsider Critical Thinking Question #1. Defend why your initial response to that question has (or has not) changed.
3. Using at least three other references (e.g., books, research-journal articles, newspaper or magazine stories or credible Web sites), write an 800- to 1,000-word essay that addresses two of the critical thinking questions offered earlier. Assume that your essay will be used as an internal reference for a government's policy guidelines.
4. Using at least three other references (e.g., books, research-journal articles, newspaper or magazine stories or credible Web sites), post an 800- to 1,000-word Web page that addresses at least two of the earlier critical thinking questions. Assume that your page will be posted in the policy section of a government's intranet.

It's Raining Farm Subsidies

By Tim Weiner

Washington—City slickers may think there was some connection between the withered cornstalks they saw on the nightly news last week and the Senate's passing a $7.4 billion "emergency" agricultural aid bill on Wednesday.

In fact, there is a crisis in American farming, but it has little to do with this summer's drought, and a lot to do with Washington.

Federal farm policy is creating bigger and bigger farms and fewer and fewer farmers, converting tens of billions of taxpayers' dollars into cattle fodder, creating big profits for the biggest agribusinesses and underwriting cheap hamburgers. But that policy is bringing precious little benefit—and, some argue, great harm—to small farmers trying to make a living, critics say.

These critics include the conservative Senator Phil Gramm of Texas, the centrist National Farmers Union, which represents 300,000 farmers and ranchers, and the liberal Environmental Defense Fund. Though they marshal their arguments in different ways, they generally agree that a system begun back in the Depression to help farmers survive is now "planting a seed that is going to destroy American agriculture as we know it," as Gramm said last week.

The Government will plow close to $24 billion into agriculture this year, assuming the Senate bill becomes law. That Federal money will account for nearly half of all farm income, Agriculture Department figures show. No other American business receives this kind of subsidy.

Very little Federal largesse goes to small farmers growing food. Most of it goes to the increasingly industrialized production of a few basic commodities like wheat, soybeans and corn—not the sweet corn of summer, but the corn that animals eat. One-third of the wheat, three-quarters of the corn and almost all the soybeans are used for feed, not food.

And much of the market for those commodities is controlled by corporations like Cargill, the nation's largest privately held company, and Archer-Daniels-Midland, the politically connected conglomerate recently fined $100 million for price-fixing. These two companies control 60 percent of the export market for American grain.

"Agriculture policy does not protect the person you or I think of as a farmer," Tom Buis of the National Farmers Union said. "It benefits the largest operations and the processors. And the processors want cheap grain. There are a lot of different interests in agriculture, and the farmers are the least powerful."

The number of small farmers—those with annual gross incomes below $250,000—has declined by 75 percent since the 1960s. With tiny profit margins, farmers must have bigger farms, pricier machines, more fertilizers, fence-to-fence plantings. Yet this often gets them nowhere. Midwestern corn farmers' gross earnings per acre are about the same as they were in 1950, though their yields have doubled, Agriculture Department figures show.

Forced to adapt or die, fewer farmers are running bigger and bigger operations. Hog barns and chicken coops become huge meat factories; these economies of scale affect farming and ranching everywhere. Farmland is concentrated in fewer and fewer hands: Five percent of the landowners now own 50 percent of all farmland.

And just as no other industry gets the kind of Federal subsidy that agriculture does, no other industry suffers from overproduction on the same scale. One big reason that prices are plummeting is that farmers are growing too much. There is no market for half this fall's wheat crop—close to a billion bushels, growers say. Federal farm law is contributing to that oversupply, the critics say. The law was revised by the Republican Congress in 1996 to remove the set-aside subsidy, which paid farmers to let part of their fields lie fallow. The old law had many critics, but the change "accelerated this trend of overproduction," said Buis. "It encouraged more production without any measures to control supply."

Tim Searchinger, a senior attorney at the Environmental Defense Fund in Washington, said: "The subsidies mean that farmers produce too many basic crops, taxpayers pay them for the excess, and farmers keep doing it. They mean millions more acres of corn and wheat fields, more tons of fertilizer and pesticides."

Before the Senate's new bill, the Agriculture Department forecast farm income declining very slightly this year, from $44.1 billion last year to $43.8 billion. Congress, by passing a bill of that size, would push the figure up above $50 billion—with $24 billion coming from the Treasury. The same forecast shows the total value of farm assets rising and farm debt declining this year.

The new farm law was supposed to let the market rule. To an extent, it has. The agribusiness giants like overproduction because it keeps prices down. But Congress pumps more and more money into the system—including a $6 billion "emergency" package last October along with the $7.4 billion offered by the Senate—and the total payout has been greater than or equal to what would have been paid under the old law, according to Agriculture Department figures cited by Searchinger.

"We are paying so much money that we are actually encouraging more production rather than compensating people partially for their losses," Senator Gramm said. "We are going to end up exacerbating oversupply and driving prices further and further down." There is a farm crisis, but it seems to be that the market, supported by the Government, is forcing America's small farmers to get big or get out.

The New York Times, August 8, 1999
http://www.nytimes.com/library/review/080899farm-aid-review.html

CRITICAL THINKING QUESTIONS

1. Should the federal government be obliged to provide subsidies to farming operations that are having financial troubles?
2. What kind of policy would you recommend to ensure that large corporate farms do not cause the demise of small farms?
3. What do you forecast for the future of small farms in America?

STORY-SPECIFIC QUESTIONS

1. What effect have recent federal farm policies had on small farms?
2. How much of a subsidy is proposed for small farms according to this story?
3. How, as indicated in this article, are subsidies harmful to taxpayers?

SHORT APPLICATION ASSIGNMENTS

1. In teams or individually, answer the story-specific questions; keep your answers to 25–75 words for each question.
2. In teams of three to five persons each, or as a whole class, discuss your responses to the critical thinking questions.
3. Prepare a one-page memo report (200–250 words) to your instructor in which you summarize this article. You will find a model one-page report on the Web site (nytimes.swcollege.com).
4. Write an executive summary (200–250 words). As an administrative assistant to a busy executive, you are expected to summarize selected articles and present important points. You will find a model executive summary on the Web site.
5. Summarize this article (100–125 words) for your company's newsletter. You will find a model newsletter on the Web site.

BUILDING RESEARCH SKILLS

1. Individually or in teams, investigate what happens to surpluses when farmers are subsidized. Your instructor may ask you to submit a three- to five-page essay, post a Web page or report your results in a five-minute presentation, along with a letter of transmittal explaining your essay.
2. Individually or in teams, review several other *New York Times* articles on farm subsidies. Your instructor may ask you to submit a three- to five-page essay, post a Web page or report your results in a five-minute presentation, along with a letter of transmittal explaining your essay. As you develop your essay, reconsider Critical Thinking Question #1. Defend why your initial response to that question has (or has not) changed.
3. Using at least three other references (e.g., books, research-journal articles, newspaper or magazine stories or credible Web sites), write an 800- to 1,000-word essay that addresses two of the critical thinking questions offered earlier. Assume that

your essay will be used as an internal reference for a government's policy guidelines.

4. Using at least three other references (e.g., books, research-journal articles, newspaper or magazine stories or credible Web sites), post an 800- to 1,000-word Web page that addresses at least two of the earlier critical thinking questions. Assume that your page will be posted in the policy section of a government's intranet.

CHAPTER 2

Macroeconomics

PREVIEW

"Macroeconomics," as an academic discipline, examines the economy as a whole; or, put simply, it frames the economic "big picture." Within the macroeconomic framework, economists analyze such problems as unemployment rates, the business cycle, monetary and fiscal policy, interest rates and inflation.

In the economic "big picture," consumers and producers are thought to behave in predictable ways. However, economists may advocate opposing views on the causes, effects and solutions to macroeconomic problems.

Richard W. Stevenson, in his article "Focus Shifts to the Central Bank's Long-Term Agenda," reviews the problems of inflation (a general increase in prices) and how the U.S. Federal Reserve Bank implements policies that attempt to stem the effects of inflationary tides. But not everyone agrees with the Federal Reserve's inflation-fighting moves. As Mr. Stevenson illustrates in "Central Bank Raises Interest Rates to Avert Inflation," a host of interested groups were quick to criticize the Fed's decision to raise interest rates during a period when inflation appeared to be under control.

In addition to questioning how the Fed can fight inflation, experts also debate the causes of inflation. Sylvia Nasar, in her article "Inflation Just Doesn't Add Up," looks at the mysterious turns in inflation and how these events may be linked to policy changes issued by the Fed.

Focus Shifts to the Central Bank's Long-Term Agenda

By Richard W. Stevenson

Washington—Is it 1994 all over again, the beginning of a prolonged series of interest rate increases intended to wring inflationary pressures out of an economy that is threatening to overheat?

Or is it 1997, when the Federal Reserve bumped interest rates up once just to let everyone know it was on the case, and then let the economy go on its rip-roaring way?

Economists and investors are all but certain that the Fed will push its benchmark lending rate up by a modest quarter of a percentage point next week in a pre-emptive strike against the possibility of resurgent inflation. And while neither 1994 nor 1997 provides a precise analogy for the current situation, what everyone wants to know is whether the central bank will be content with a tap or two on the monetary brakes to reassert its inflation-fighting credibility, or whether the Fed will embark on a more vigorous series of rate increases.

Alan Greenspan, the Fed chairman, hinted in congressional testimony last week that the central bank itself did not know yet how far it would have to go to deny inflation a foothold, and would decide based on how the economy performed in coming months.

"What we try to do is make the best judgments we can at the particular time that we meet, or if it is relevant, between meetings," Greenspan told the Joint Economic Committee. "I don't recall ever having a sense that we are going to do a series of increases or decreases."

Still, assuming no significant acceleration or slowdown in economic activity over the next few months, the odds now seem to favor an in-between scenario in which the Fed tightens its benchmark federal funds target rate by a quarter point next week, to 5 percent, and then perhaps once more by another quarter point later in the summer, before shifting back into neutral.

Although the economy has repeatedly proved to be far stronger than analysts predicted the last several years, many economists think the combination of two modest rate increases by the Fed, combined with the rise the last few months in long-term rates set by the bond market, should be enough to slow the economy to a point where inflation recedes as a threat.

"The view the market has now, and we agree with it, is that another rate hike is coming, but that this round of tightening will not have to be aggressive," said James Glassman, an economist at Chase Securities in New York.

"The market now seems priced for another quarter-point move in August, and that's it for a while until we see how things work out."

The judgments made by Greenspan and his colleagues in coming months will be among the trickiest they have faced in several years. While they now appear comfortable shifting their attention from financial conditions around the world back to the situation in the United States, Greenspan in particular will have to balance his oft-expressed belief in the inflation-dampening power of increased productivity against his fear of endangering the domestic price stability of the last few years.

For all the obvious comparisons, policy-makers may draw little guidance from their experiences raising rates in 1994 and 1997. While the Fed, for example, also acted in 1994 to head off inflation before it took root, it started at a time when monetary policy was far looser than it is today. The Fed funds rate stood at just 3 percent when, in February 1994, the central bank made the first of seven increases that over the course of a year doubled the rate to 6 percent.

The Fed's immediate goal this time around is not so much to squelch inflation—there is almost no inflation—as it is to head off the forces that can create inflation. Although a rebound in oil prices has helped push the Consumer Price Index up somewhat this year, the one-month spike in April of seven-tenths of a percent is now widely viewed as an aberration, and by most measures prices remained stable last month.

"For the time being, inflation remains exceptionally quiescent, with the year-over-year increase in consumer prices, excluding food and energy, falling to 2.1 percent, the lowest rate in more than 30 years," economists at Goldman, Sachs told clients in a report this week.

The Fed's somewhat more nebulous target is demand for goods and services, which has been running at consistently robust levels. In the view of most Fed officials, the combination of strong demand growth and extremely low unemployment is potentially volatile. Left unchecked, they say, strong demand will ultimately force companies to bid up wages to find the employees they need in a dwindling pool of available workers—and rising wages could ultimately lead companies to raise prices, setting off an inflationary spiral.

But the trick for the Fed will be to temper demand without setting off a destabilizing rout on Wall Street, where ever-higher stock prices have left many consumers feeling flush and willing to spend. And the Fed will have to act in the face of opposition from some members of both parties who say the central bank is sacrificing jobs and wage increases in pursuit of a problem that does not exist.

"If we make policy on the basis of the fear of inflation, we will inevitably forgo the very benefits that have been so crucially important to working families these last three years," John Sweeney, the president of the AFL-CIO, told a news conference on Capitol Hill Thursday.

One way that Fed officials and economists generally are framing the debate is to compare the economy and monetary policy last summer to conditions today.

Last summer, before the global financial crisis became acute and began threatening markets in the United States, the Fed's benchmark federal funds target rate stood at 5.5 percent—three-quarters of a percentage point higher than today's—and the central bank was leaning toward pushing rates higher. Only the need to stabilize markets at home and around the world led the Fed to reverse policy and cut rates three times in the fall in quarter-point increments.

Now, with the global crisis apparently past and demand from both Europe and Japan likely to pick up, one camp of economists makes the case that if a Fed funds rate of 5.5 percent or higher was appropriate last summer, it is appropriate now.

After all, unemployment, which was 4.5 percent last August, has declined to 4.2 percent. Growth in gross domestic product, which was 3.7 percent in the summer quarter last year, jumped to 6 percent later in the year and remained a torrid 4.1 percent in this year's first quarter. And the Dow Jones industrial average, which stood at around 8,500 just before the financial crisis flared last August, closed Thursday at 10,534.83, a jump of nearly 24 percent.

John Makin, an economist at the American Enterprise Institute, said a series of rate increases now could be seen as a continuation of a tightening policy that began not last summer but as far back as March 1997, when the Fed pushed rates up by a quarter point, to 5.5 percent. Only the initial outbreak of the Asian crisis in the summer of 1997 and the steady spread of financial problems around the world the next year, he said, kept the Fed from tightening further in that period.

"This string of unprecedented financial shocks can be viewed as an interruption in a Fed process of tightening in response to strong U.S. demand growth initiated over two years ago," Makin said in a recent report. "Given that it was on track to tighten in spring 1997, the Fed would be reasonable to contemplate taking back the 75 basis points of easing last fall in response to systemic risk."

But another group of economists, influenced in part by Greenspan, points out that the economy today is not the same as last summer's—that the most significant changes since then are an increase in the growth of productivity, or output for each hour worked, and a deceleration in the pace of wage increases despite the declining unemployment rate.

Both factors suggest that the economy is less inflation prone than it was last summer. The rise in productivity means companies can offset cost increases with improved efficiency rather than price increases. And the drop-off in wage growth suggests that workers are not using the leverage of a tight labor market to win big raises, possibly because of a deeply ingrained fear that they could lose their jobs to global competition and possibly because employers are compensating workers with performance-based bonuses.

"There's less skepticism now than last summer about the favorable inflation outlook," Glassman said. "The more we see what's happening around the globe, and the more we see what's happening with productivity, the more open-minded people are about the economy's ability to sustain low inflation. That argues that the Fed does not have to push rates back up to where they were."

Greenspan made clear in his congressional testimony last week that his primary concern is not the heady level of the stock market, as worrisome as that is to him, but the possible effect of continued strong domestic demand on wages.

But it is difficult to make an ironclad case these days that rising wages will lead to a general increase in prices. So far, productivity gains have more than offset rising wages and other costs. The problem, as Greenspan has noted repeatedly, is that policy-makers cannot count on productivity growth to continue to improve forever. At some point, the productivity growth rate could level off, or wage growth could accelerate, and the seeds of inflation would then take root in the form of rising cost structures within companies.

Yet even if that happens, it is by no means certain that companies will be able to pass on their higher costs to consumers because competition is so intense that producers have proved to be willing to give up profits to maintain or gain market share.

Moreover, there is little evidence of any acceleration in wage increases in the first place.

"The pressure on labor costs is milder than we thought it would be, despite the fact that the economy is stronger," said Richard Rippe, an economist at Prudential Securities in New York.

Rippe said there were other reasons why the Fed was unlikely to raise rates aggressively the rest of the year. The domestic economy is already showing some tentative signs of slowing.

While the global crisis appears past, the recoveries in many countries are fragile and could be hurt by higher rates in the United States. And Rippe said the Fed would like to avoid driving the value of the dollar higher, which would be likely if interest rates in the United States rose substantially. While a stronger dollar would help contain inflation by holding down import prices, it could also lead to a further expansion of the trade deficit, which is not yet a major problem but could ultimately become one.

The New York Times, June 25, 1999
http://www.nytimes.com/library/financial/fed/062599interest-rates.html

CRITICAL THINKING QUESTIONS

1. Explain why the actions taken by the Fed to keep inflation down are very important.
2. Do you think the rise in the number of people investing in the stock market has worked as an anti-inflation mechanism? Why, or why not?
3. Does the Fed have too much power over the U.S. economy? Why, or why not?

STORY-SPECIFIC QUESTIONS

1. Why is the Fed contemplating raising interest rates?
2. What explanation is given for the decline in wage increases?
3. Explain the global effects of higher interest rates and a stronger dollar.

SHORT APPLICATION ASSIGNMENTS

1. In teams or individually, answer the story-specific questions; keep your answers to 25–75 words for each question.
2. In teams of three to five persons each, or as a whole class, discuss your responses to the critical thinking questions.
3. Prepare a one-page memo report (200–250 words) to your instructor in which you summarize this article. You will find a model one-page report on the Web site (nytimes.swcollege.com).
4. Write an executive summary (200–250 words). As an administrative assistant to a busy executive, you are expected to summarize selected articles and present important points. You will find a model executive summary on the Web site.
5. Summarize this article (100–125 words) for your company's newsletter. You will find a model newsletter on the Web site.

BUILDING RESEARCH SKILLS

1. Individually or in teams, visit the Federal Bureau of Labor Statistics' Web site (http://stats.bls.gov/) to research the Consumer Price Index (CPI) and the Producer Price Index (PPI) as they relate to monitoring consumer spending habits. What kinds of consumer behavior patterns are you able to recognize from both indexes? Why could each index influence policies related to inflation? Your instructor may ask you to submit a three- to five-page essay, post a Web page or report your results in a five-minute presentation, along with a letter of transmittal explaining your essay.
2. Using at least three other references (e.g., books, research-journal articles, newspaper or magazine stories or credible Web sites), write an 800- to 1,000-word essay that addresses two of the critical thinking questions offered earlier. Assume that your essay will be used as an internal reference for a government's policy guidelines.
3. Using at least three other references (e.g., books, research-journal articles, newspaper or magazine stories or credible Web sites), post an 800- to 1,000-word Web page that addresses at least two of the earlier critical thinking questions. Assume that your page will be posted in the policy section of a government's intranet.

Central Bank Raises Interest Rates to Avert Inflation

By Richard W. Stevenson

The Federal Reserve raised interest rates on Tuesday by a quarter of a percentage point, the second increase in less than two months, saying the action should help avert inflation while allowing the nation's long economic expansion to continue.

Brushing aside arguments from farmers, labor unions, manufacturers and some politicians that there was no inflation to fight, the central bank said it would increase the main rate it controls, the Federal funds target rate on overnight loans among banks, to 5.25 percent from 5 percent. It also said it would raise its more symbolic discount rate on loans to banks from the Federal Reserve system to 4.75 percent from 4.5 percent.

The Fed said the risks of inflation should now be "markedly" diminished, a statement that investors and analysts read to suggest that further rate increases this year, while by no means out of the question, were less likely.

Although relatively small, Tuesday's increases were intended to slow the economy by putting upward pressure on borrowing costs, or at least to help lock in a general rise over much of this year in the rates set by the financial markets. Mortgage rates, for example, have risen substantially this year, but their future course will depend largely on the bond markets' assessment of the risks of inflation and higher interest rates.

Banks quickly raised their prime lending rates to 8.25 percent from 8 percent, a step that will result in higher rates on some consumer and small business loans.

Stocks seesawed after the Fed's announcement and ended the day mixed. But analysts said the hint that further rate increases might not be necessary was good news for investors, who have bid stock prices up to record levels recently on the assumption that the central bank could control inflation without a protracted series of rate increases. Apparently driven by that reasoning, bond prices rose today, pushing long-term rates down slightly.

In a statement, the Fed portrayed its decision as another step in reversing the three quarter-point rate cuts it made last fall, when the global financial system was threatening to seize up and other countries were looking to the United States for help in keeping their economies afloat.

The global crisis has largely passed, and in the meantime the American economy has continued to expand robustly, setting off some tentative warning signals about inflation but generating almost no actual inflation so far.

Having now taken back two of last fall's three rate cuts, the Fed distinctly left open the possibility that it could raise rates a third time this year. Economists said the central bank could still increase rates another notch at its next meeting on October 5 or the subsequent meeting on Nov. 16 if economic data showed inflationary pressure in the form of a sharp decline in unemployment, further big wage increases or a substantial rise in the Consumer Price Index.

But its statement suggested that the Fed saw its work as more likely to be finished for the year, with any threat of inflation now contained.

"You'd have to view the odds of an Oct. 5 rate hike as considerably less than 50-50 at this point," said Bill Dudley, an economist at Goldman, Sachs in New York. "Obviously it depends on the data, but most likely the Fed is done for the year."

The Fed's statement said that with financial markets having recovered, economies worldwide bouncing back and strong growth in the United States creating an extremely tight labor market, "the degree of monetary ease required to address the global financial market turmoil of last fall is no longer consistent with sustained, noninflationary economic expansion."

In what analysts said was an important shift in tone by the central bank, the statement added that the combination of the two rate increases by the Fed plus a rise in recent months in the longer-term rates set by the markets "should markedly diminish the risk of rising inflation going forward."

The central bank said it had adopted a neutral outlook about the need for any changes to monetary policy over the short run, meaning that it did not see any clear evidence now that it would have to raise rates again. But it is unclear how much value that stance has in predicting the Fed's decision when it meets in October because it adopted a neutral position after raising rates a quarter-point on June 30 and went on to raise rates again today.

The central bank's action drew criticism from a variety of interest groups and politicians who traditionally oppose higher rates.

They said on Tuesday that the increase was unjustified at a time when overall inflation was nearly dormant and the prices of farm products and some other commodities were falling or depressed. They said most companies had little ability to raise prices because of intense competition and had proved determined to absorb cost increases by increasing their efficiency.

"At a time when inflation is almost dormant and when foreign markets are only now beginning to emerge from recession, this decision is a disappointment," said Jerry Jasinowski, the president of the National Association of Manufacturers.

Representative Barney Frank, Democrat of Massachusetts, said the rate increase would "increase the likelihood that our national economic progress will continue to fail to benefit fully those at the lower end of the economic spectrum." Steve Forbes, the Republican Presidential candidate, said the Fed was turning a mighty economy into "the economic equivalent of the Titanic."

But economists on Wall Street said the Fed was doing the right thing to fight inflation before it took root because price stability has been the foundation on which the long expansion has been built.

"I'm right with the Fed on this issue," said Allen Sinai, an economist at Primark Decision Economics in New York, adding that the central bank had to act early because "inflation is a glacial process, loaded with inertia."

As it has for the last several years, the Fed's Federal Open Market Committee came into today's meeting facing a raft of somewhat contradictory economic data.

Although it slowed in the second quarter and faces potential trouble from a rapidly expanding trade deficit and a weakening dollar, the economy appears to have regained momentum over the summer. Industrial output last month rose to its highest rate in more than a year. Housing starts remain strong and retail sales are robust. Demand for imports was strong, and rebounding economies in Asia and Europe mean better prospects for exporters.

With growth strong, job creation has remained brisk, and wages rose last month at a pace that while gratifying to workers was seen by some economists as the first signs of a possible inflationary spiral. Alan Greenspan, the Fed chairman, has repeatedly focused in his public comments on the depletion of the labor pool and the possibility of an excessive surge in wages as the most immediate inflationary threat to the economy.

Still, inflation by nearly all measures has remained controlled, if not dormant, leaving the Fed in the position of fighting what critics consider a phantom menace.

The Fed has had to weigh several other tricky issues in setting policy. It would clearly prefer not to have to raise rates later this year at a time when the Year 2000 computer problem could be having real or psychological effects on the economy and the financial markets. Some analysts said the Fed might have decided to tighten policy today to reduce the need to do so late in the year.

The central bank also continues to grapple with the relentless rise in stock prices, seeing both a threat to financial stability in the possibility of a market crash and a "wealth effect" that fuels consumption at a time when the Fed is trying to slow the economy.

Rising interest rates generally dampen enthusiasm among investors, but Wall Street has so far been undaunted by the two rate increases, at least partly offsetting any slowdown the higher rates might bring.

The New York Times, August 25, 1999
http://www.nytimes.com/library/financial/fed/082599fed-rates.html

CRITICAL THINKING QUESTIONS

1. Explain the effects of increased productivity/output on inflation.
2. Do you think the Fed should have the exclusive responsibility of raising interest rates as it sees fit?
3. What do you foresee as long-term consequences of raising interest rates?

STORY-SPECIFIC QUESTIONS

1. Why did the Fed raise interest rates twice in two months?
2. How did the increase in interest rates affect the stock market?
3. Explain the Fed's "neutral" position following its rate increase.

SHORT APPLICATION ASSIGNMENTS

1. In teams or individually, answer the story-specific questions; keep your answers to 25–75 words for each question.
2. In teams of three to five persons each, or as a whole class, discuss your responses to the critical thinking questions.
3. Prepare a one-page memo report (200–250 words) to your instructor in which you summarize this article. You will find a model one-page report on the Web site (nytimes.swcollege.com).
4. Write an executive summary (200–250 words). As an administrative assistant to a busy executive, you are expected to summarize selected articles and present important points. You will find a model executive summary on the Web site.
5. Summarize this article (100–125 words) for your company's newsletter. You will find a model newsletter on the Web site.

BUILDING RESEARCH SKILLS

1. Individually or in teams, investigate the last two interest rate moves by the Federal Reserve. Why did the Fed raise or lower interest rates? Which rates did the Fed raise or lower? Did the Fed change its bias? Your instructor may ask you to submit a three- to five-page essay, post a Web page or report your results in a five-minute presentation, along with a letter of transmittal explaining your essay.
2. Using at least three other references (e.g., books, research-journal articles, newspaper or magazine stories or credible Web sites), write an 800- to 1,000-word essay that addresses two of the critical thinking questions offered earlier. Assume that your essay will be used as an internal reference for a government's policy guidelines.
3. Using at least three other references (e.g., books, research-journal articles, newspaper or magazine stories or credible Web sites), post an 800- to 1,000-word Web page that addresses at least two of the earlier critical thinking questions. Assume that your page will be posted in the policy section of a government's intranet.

Inflation Just Doesn't Add Up

By Sylvia Nasar

Barely a year after a worldwide deflation scare—when markets and currencies were crashing, banks and businesses in Asia, Russia and Latin America were failing, and prices of oil and raw materials were plunging—inflation is back on peoples' minds.

On the face of it, fretting about inflation when every major price gauge in the United States is rising just 2 percent or so a year seems a little like Uma Thurman obsessing over her weight. But what concerns Alan Greenspan, the Federal Reserve chairman, and Wall Street investors is the nagging suspicion that the stellar inflation record of the last two years was mostly the product of a few lucky, highly transitory breaks—and therefore won't last. That suspicion is likely to propel the Fed's policy-making committee toward another interest-rate increase when it meets on Tuesday.

Admittedly, the budding recovery in Asia and Europe has already blunted some of the forces that have helped push U.S. inflation down from 4 percent to 2 percent a year since 1997. Energy prices—indeed, most commodity prices other than farm products—are already rebounding sharply after collapsing last year. And the high-flying dollar, which helped to make imports cheaper, has recently weakened against the euro and the yen as global investors have begun to shift some of their mutual fund money away from the United States to foreign markets.

Sounds dire, right? Actually, there are solid reasons for thinking that a return to the bad old days, when upwardly spiraling prices seemed as inevitable as the sunrise, is highly unlikely. For one thing, some of those "transitory" factors are likely to persist for quite a while longer. For another, popular expectations about inflation—low inflation, this time—readily become self-fulfilling prophecies. And a host of structural and policy changes over the last couple of decades have made the U.S. economy less inherently prone to inflation.

Even skeptics now say that the low inflation of the 1990s is not just a fluke, but rather a return to a norm that prevailed for a quarter-century, beginning in the late 1940s—years when 4 percent inflation seemed scandalously high. As Alan S. Blinder, an economist at Princeton University and former vice chairman of the Federal Reserve, said recently, "To a substantial extent, we're back to the '50s."

Jeffrey Frankel of Harvard University, until recently a member of the President's Council of Economic Advisers, said of mainstream economists: "A lot of us were real stick-in-the-muds. We said: 'No, no, no. Here are the equations.' But other people who knew less about equations had the sense to realize that things are a bit different."

For starters, not all the good luck is evaporating. True, energy prices have jumped 24 percent since the beginning of the year. But energy wasn't a big factor in inflation's decline—the economy uses a lot less energy than it did in, say, 1973—and this year's price increase isn't anything like the surges in 1973 or 1990. Most of the impact has already filtered through to consumer prices for gasoline, electricity, heating oil and air fares, adding at most a few tenths of a percentage point to the inflation rate.

The dollar's recent dip and the ballooning trade deficit have some economists, notably Paul Krugman of the Massachusetts Institute of Technology, warning of the possibility of a currency crisis. If the dollar were to take a big dive, that would indeed threaten to push inflation up sharply. But it would also provoke a sharp reaction from the Fed. And the dollar is still slightly stronger on a trade-weighted basis (that is, against a basket of currencies of America's trading partners) than it was at the start of the year.

More to the point, import prices, by far the biggest recent drag on inflation, are apt to remain under downward pressure. Their decline, it turns out, was due less to the strong dollar than to vast excess productive capacity in Asia, Latin America and elsewhere—an excess that will not be mopped up soon, given the gradual pace of world recovery. "It's not just the dollar, but economic incentives to increase production abroad," said Robert J. Gordon, an economist at Northwestern University.

Domestically, health care costs have stopped skyrocketing and show few signs of resuming that course, despite increases over the last year in the fees that health maintenance organizations charge employers. Though the latest readings show consumer prices for medical care rising a bit faster than a year ago, few experts expect the pace to accelerate to twice the overall inflation rate, as it did in the early 1990s.

In any case, even temporary lulls in inflation can have long-term effects, by changing expectations. Americans who believed two decades ago that inflation would always rise are now expecting it to remain low. According to the monthly University of Michigan survey of consumer expectations, ordinary Americans expect the inflation rate a year from now to be under 3 percent. (The Federal Reserve forecasts 2.5 percent or less.) "You get this extra impact," Gordon said. "The biggest factor holding down inflation in the next couple of years is the lower inflation of the past couple."

But perhaps the strongest reasons for optimism are sweeping changes in the economy that have been in the works for years.

Back in the bad old 1970s, temporary supply shocks tended to produce higher inflation automatically. Since then, some long-term trends—globalization, deregulation, the computer revolution—have made the economy less susceptible to bottlenecks and wage-price spirals. "One story is that we are permanently able to run the economy hotter and labor markets tighter," Krugman said, "because we have a more flexible labor market, and monopoly and union power have been curbed by international competition."

Consider deregulation, which began during the Carter administration and has since radically transformed broad swaths of the sprawling service sector, including airlines, energy, banking, railroads, telecommunications and, most recently, electricity. More competition helps rein in inflation directly, and a new wealth of alternatives keeps strikes or other disruptions from creating bottle-necks. (Remember what life was like before faxes, cell phones and e-mail?) "They all kind of connect the economy together," Frankel said.

Then there's the computer revolution. Information technology helps com-panies do everything they do—notably, managing inventory—more flexibly and efficiently. But innovation is also driving down computer prices, and rap-idly enough to take half a percentage point off the overall inflation rate, ac-cording to Gordon.

More prosaic changes in the way the American labor market works may be as important as globalization. Alan B. Krueger of Princeton University and Lawrence F. Katz of Harvard recently published a study suggesting that a host of small, incremental changes—including the decline of unions, the growing role of temporary-help firms, even welfare reform—have made the labor mar-ket more efficient. That may be why an unemployment rate below the prevail-ing average of the 1950s and 1960s has yet to set off bidding wars among em-ployers.

And though the labor market may be tight, American business is still oper-ating with a lot of spare capacity, the product of an investment boom spurred by lower interest rates and a rush to embrace technology. Utilization rates re-main relatively low even after eight years of economic expansion—one reason that companies find it hard to raise prices. "That could explain why inflation is lower than you'd think just looking at unemployment," Frankel said.

That investment boom has had another powerful anti-inflation effect. Pro-ductivity has been growing at around 2 percent a year, double the rate that pre-vailed in the 1970s and 1980s. Greater efficiency, in turn, has made it possible for employers to increase compensation at a higher pace than the inflation rate without adding much to their costs. "We've had an acceleration of productiv-ity growth, and it takes a while before people build that expectation into wages," Krugman said.

Of course, even the most open, flexible, productive economy can suffer inflation. Inflation, as Milton Friedman, the Nobel Prize-winning economist, has said, is ultimately a monetary phenomenon, and is therefore determined by policy makers in Washington, most notably the Fed. Recall how the low-inflation post-war era ended: tax cuts and guns-and-butter spending under Presidents Kennedy and Johnson and an accommodating central bank let the inflation genie out of the bottle even before the Organization of Petroleum Exporting Countries quadrupled oil prices in 1973.

Putting the genie back in the bottle cost the nation a couple of nasty reces-sions and years of high unemployment and lost output. Today, the memory of the high human and political costs of wringing inflation out of the system helps keep inflation at bay, much as memories of the Great Depression have kept deflation at bay. Three times in 10 years, Alan Greenspan has struck preemptively with interest-rate increases to ward off any acceleration before it could even begin, in 1989, 1994 and now—strikes that so far, at least, seem to have served the economy well.

The New York Times, August 22, 1999
http://www.nytimes.com/library/financial/fed/082299econ-inflation.html

CRITICAL THINKING QUESTIONS

1. Explain the impact of medical costs on inflation. Explain the side effects of energy prices on inflation.
2. How does the economic rebound in Asia and Europe influence inflation in the United States?
3. Explain how improved efficiency with the use of technology in production is (or isn't) the key to America's increased productivity.

STORY-SPECIFIC QUESTIONS

1. How much of an impact have import prices had on inflation?
2. What do most Americans believe about the future of inflation? Explain.

SHORT APPLICATION ASSIGNMENTS

1. In teams or individually, answer the story-specific questions; keep your answers to 25–75 words for each question.
2. In teams of three to five persons each, or as a whole class, discuss your responses to the critical thinking questions.
3. Prepare a one-page memo report (200–250 words) to your instructor in which you summarize this article. You will find a model one-page report on the Web site (nytimes.swcollege.com).
4. Write an executive summary (200–250 words). As an administrative assistant to a busy executive, you are expected to summarize selected articles and present important points. You will find a model executive summary on the Web site.
5. Summarize this article (100–125 words) for your company's newsletter. You will find a model newsletter on the Web site.

BUILDING RESEARCH SKILLS

1. Individually or in teams, research the *New York Times* special section on the Federal Reserve (http://www.nytimes.com/library/financial/fed/index-fed.html). Identify and summarize at least two articles supporting or defending either monetarist or Keynesian views on steps for slowing or stopping inflation. Your instructor may ask you to

submit a three- to five-page essay, post a Web page or report your results in a five-minute presentation, along with a letter of transmittal explaining your essay.

2. Using at least three other references (e.g., books, research-journal articles, newspaper or magazine stories or credible Web sites), write an 800- to 1,000-word essay that addresses two of the critical thinking questions offered earlier. Assume that your essay will be used as an internal reference for a government's policy guidelines.

3. Using at least three other references (e.g., books, research-journal articles, newspaper or magazine stories or credible Web sites), post an 800- to 1,000-word Web page that addresses at least two of the earlier critical thinking questions. Assume that your page will be posted in the policy section of a government's intranet.

CHAPTER 3

Microeconomics

PREVIEW

Wwhen economists study individual pieces—or the many "small pictures"—of a nation's economy, they are conducting "microeconomic analysis." For instance, microeconomics includes marketplace decisions made by firms or individuals. Among other things, microeconomic analysis tends to focus on business organization, labor markets, consumer choice, consumer demand and market models. And it goes beyond business issues and could examine voter activity or public-choice issues, for example.

The first two articles in this chapter focus on business organization and structure, and the problems associated with big companies creating monopolistic strongholds on product markets. Specifically, Microsoft has been under increasing scrutiny by U.S. government antitrust regulators because of the behemoth's influence on the computer software market. As characterized by Microsoft's success, the most difficult problem of antitrust enforcement is found in industries where the producing unit is so large that only a few firms are necessary in the entire industry.

In "Antitrust in the Slow Lane," Steve Lohr examines the concerns and policy issues that antitrust regulators confront in the fast-paced technology industry. Next, Joel Brinkley writes about reactions in the high-tech industry and the anticipated

Robin Edwards, a janitor and mother of six, hit Wisconsin's welfare deadline but got an extension.

Source: Nicole Bengiveno/The New York Times

consequences of an antitrust judgment against Microsoft in his article, "U.S. Judge Declares Microsoft a Monopoly That Stifles Industry." Jason DeParle investigates the public-choice issues associated with government welfare policy in "As Welfare Benefits Expire, Second Thoughts," which highlights the real-life consequences of microeconomic policy.

Antitrust in the Slow Lane

By Steve Lohr

The outcome of the government's suit against Microsoft, filed 14 months ago, is still far from certain, and the endgame may be two or three years away, after appeals that may well reach the Supreme Court.

But one byproduct is already evident: a policy debate over whether the current system of antitrust enforcement, dating back to Theodore Roosevelt and the railway barons, is up to the challenge of policing corporate behavior in a modern, high-technology economy.

The issue is speed, the stakes are high and the debate is often highly politicized. In June, Dick Armey, the House majority leader, issued his statement of principles for government's role in an economy increasingly powered by silicon, software and the Internet. Called "An E-Contract with High-Tech America," it warned against "allowing antitrust law to become an excuse for bureaucratic interference with innovation and competition."

In a scarcely veiled reference to the Microsoft case, it criticized federal agencies that "use heavy-handed tactics to target specific companies." And it said "the pace of innovation is so quick" that market power—with which antitrust law concerns itself—is often fleeting. Armey's staff says no new antitrust bill is now planned but calls the E-Contract a "starting point."

To be sure, the Armey document can be seen as a predictable gesture from a conservative Republican leader, especially as an election year looms and Microsoft is becoming a more active campaign contributor. But you don't have to side with Bill Gates to see legitimate concerns about whether the government's antitrust police and the courts can keep up with such fast-moving industries.

A Justice Department advisory committee of executives, academics and lawyers raised that issue in a meeting last month. Committee members said the discussion was not about Microsoft, but rather about the best antitrust policies in an environment of rapid technological obsolescence. Among the options pondered were new guidelines for the Justice Department and the Federal Trade Commission and "clearer, cleaner definitions" of forbidden behavior in new legislation.

The goal is up-to-date ground rules for powerful companies like Microsoft and Intel, which settled its own antitrust dispute with the FTC earlier this year. "Policy-making has to be streamlined so it can operate on something closer to Internet time, as these industries do," said David B. Yoffie, a professor at Harvard Business School and a committee member.

The rapid pace of change in the software industry will not much affect the verdict on the legality of Microsoft's business practices. But when cases drag on as Microsoft's has, the speed issue weighs heavily on the remedies prosecutors seek. No ruling on Microsoft is expected from the federal district court in Washington before the end of the year, 18 months after the suit was filed. Again, you needn't be a Microsoft ally to notice how much has changed since the case began: Microsoft's main corporate "victim" in the case, Netscape Communications, has been acquired by America Online, and its former chief executive, James L. Barksdale, is now a venture capitalist and enthusiastic backer of George W. Bush, who, if elected President, might see antitrust policy somewhat differently than the Clinton administration has.

The speed issue figures prominently in the chess game of settlement discussions between Microsoft and the government. Joel I. Klein, head of the Justice Department's antitrust division, will say only that the settlement equation is "time versus risk." A settlement would rein in Microsoft sooner than a verdict would, Klein said, but the negotiated terms might leave Microsoft enough leeway to abuse its market power.

By judicial standards, the Microsoft case has moved with surprising speed: "a remarkable achievement," according to Andrew I. Gavil, a law professor at Howard University, writing in *Antitrust* magazine, an American Bar Association journal. Judge Thomas Penfield Jackson, Gavil said, has used innovative tactics—from requiring all direct testimony in writing to limiting the number of witnesses—to speed the proceedings along and avoid the "prolonged trench warfare" that has plagued major cases like the government's suit against IBM, which was dropped in 1982, after 13 years.

But even the most expeditious courts are too slow in many eyes, part of the reason so many antitrust cases are settled. "It may be fast compared with the IBM case, but it's not fast enough, and that's a problem," said Carl Shapiro, an economist at the University of California at Berkeley and a former senior Justice Department official. "A lot of things do change in 18 months."

The New York Times, July 11, 1999
http://www.nytimes.com/library/tech/99/07/biztech/articles/11antitrust.html

CRITICAL THINKING QUESTIONS

1. How do you think the verdict will impact the software industry?
2. Why do you suppose it is so important to draw a speedy decision in the case?
3. Is Microsoft a monopoly? Why, or why not?

STORY-SPECIFIC QUESTIONS

1. What position do Dick Armey and other conservatives take regarding the bureaucratic presence in the technology industry?
2. How, according to this article, does rapidly changing technology impact the Microsoft case?

3. What measures have been taken by Judge Jackson to successfully hasten a decision in the Microsoft case with regard to the Microsoft and antitrust litigation?

SHORT APPLICATION ASSIGNMENTS

1. In teams or individually, answer the story-specific questions; keep your answers to 25–75 words for each question.
2. In teams of three to five persons each, or as a whole class, discuss your responses to the critical thinking questions.
3. Prepare a one-page memo report (200–250 words) to your instructor in which you summarize this article. You will find a model one-page report on the Web site (nytimes.swcollege.com).
4. Write an executive summary (200–250 words). As an administrative assistant to a busy executive, you are expected to summarize selected articles and present important points. You will find a model executive summary on the Web site.
5. Summarize this article (100–125 words) for your company's newsletter. You will find a model newsletter on the Web site.

BUILDING RESEARCH SKILLS

1. Individually or in teams, research various antitrust laws including the Sherman Act (1890), the FTC Act (1914) and the Hart-Scott-Rodino Antitrust Improvement Act (1980). Prepare a proposed antitrust law that would suitably focus on the Microsoft antitrust lawsuit. What language would you include from previous legislation? What language from previous antitrust acts would be unsuitable for Microsoft and others in the industry? What measures in your legislation would guarantee industry compliance? Your instructor may ask you to submit a three- to five-page essay, post a Web page or report your results in a five-minute presentation, along with a letter of transmittal explaining your essay.
2. Individually or in teams, research the current status of the Microsoft antitrust lawsuit. Your instructor may ask you to submit a three- to five-page essay, post a Web page or report your results in a five-minute presentation, along with a letter of transmittal explaining your essay.
3. Using at least three other references (e.g., books, research-journal articles, newspaper or magazine stories or credible Web sites), write an 800- to 1,000-word essay that addresses two of the critical thinking questions offered earlier. Assume that your essay will be used as an internal reference for a government's policy guidelines.
4. Using at least three other references (e.g., books, research-journal articles, newspaper or magazine stories or credible Web sites), post an 800- to 1,000-word Web page that addresses at least two of the earlier critical thinking questions. Assume that your page will be posted in the policy section of a government's intranet.

U.S. Judge Declares Microsoft a Monopoly That Stifles Industry

By Joel Brinkley

Washington—The judge in the government's antitrust trial against the Microsoft Corporation issued a broad denunciation of the software giant Friday evening as the first part of his verdict in the landmark case.

The judge, Thomas Penfield Jackson of Federal District Court, said the company had used its monopoly power to stifle innovation, reduce competition and hurt consumers.

"Most harmful of all is the message that Microsoft's actions have conveyed to every enterprise with the potential to innovate in the computer industry," Judge Jackson wrote in his 207-page findings of fact.

"Through its conduct," he added, "Microsoft has demonstrated that it will use its prodigious market power and immense profits to harm any firm that insists on pursuing initiatives that could intensify competition against one of Microsoft's core products."

Judge Jackson's findings of fact are not a final verdict but a declaration of which side's version of events he believes. They clearly show that he found the government's case against Microsoft credible and rejected as "specious," as he stated in one part, virtually all the arguments Microsoft put up in its defense.

The findings are the judge's conclusions about who presented the most compelling and believable case during the yearlong trial that opened in his U.S. district courtroom on October 19, 1998. As such, they clearly signal how he will rule in his eventual verdict.

Microsoft and the government both reacted quickly after receiving the much-anticipated findings this evening. The judge, who in years past wrote his decisions longhand, transmitted the document to both sides by e-mail this afternoon. It was made public at 6:30 P.M., after the stock markets had closed.

In after-hours trading, Microsoft closed down more than $4, at $87, on the Island ECN, compared with its closing price of $91.5625 during the regular session on the Nasdaq. It was trading at $87.75 on Instinet.

The Justice Department was jubilant. "This is a great day for American consumers," Attorney General Janet Reno said. "This case is about the protection of innovation, competition and the consumers' right to choose the products they want."

Microsoft, on the other hand, quickly issued a statement indicating that the company was already formulating its appeal.

"While we disagree with many of the findings," the statement said, "we are still confident that the law supports us on these points and that the American legal system will ultimately rule that Microsoft's actions were fair, legal and good for consumers."

Later, Microsoft's chairman, William H. Gates, said: "We respectfully disagree with the court's findings. Microsoft competes vigorously and fairly. Microsoft is committed to resolving this case in a fair and equitable manner." He added that his company "operates within the laws and operates in a way that is great for the people we develop software for."

Neither in Microsoft's statements nor those of the Justice Department, was there much talk of settling the case. Joel I. Klein, head of the Justice Department's antitrust division, said the government would consider a settlement, but only one that "fully and properly addresses" the issues raised in the judge's findings.

Although the judge's findings of fact are virtually impervious to appeal, Microsoft's leaders are expected to seek grounds for appeal, should Judge Jackson eventually rule against them.

Under federal court rules, appeals courts must give great weight to the conclusions the trial judge draws from hearing the testimony and studying the witnesses as they offer their accounts.

As a result, appeals courts are allowed to challenge findings of fact only if they are "clearly erroneous." And if the judge's verdict is largely based on which witnesses he believed, the verdict stands a better chance of withstanding appeal.

At the outset of his findings, the judge declared that Microsoft "enjoys monopoly power in the relevant market." This is a key assertion because under antitrust laws monopolies cannot engage in practices that would be legal for other companies. The government's charges rested on the assumption that Microsoft has a monopoly in the operating systems market with its Windows operating systems.

In a key test for monopoly power, Judge Jackson concluded that Microsoft could charge whatever it wanted for Windows without fear that price increases would reduce demand.

Microsoft expended considerable energy in court arguing that it was not a monopoly.

It asserted that a host of small competitors—from the Be operating system to Palm Pilot personal organizers—were long-term threats. But Judge Jackson dismissed those arguments, saying that competition from those competitors was, at the very least, a long way off.

"That day has not arrived, nor does it seem imminent," he wrote of one such claim.

"Microsoft's monopoly power," he concluded, "is also evidenced by the fact that, over the course of several years, Microsoft took actions that only could have been advantageous if they operated to reinforce monopoly power."

From there, the judge ran through each of the charges raised by the Justice

Department and the 19 state attorneys general who joined in the suit. In each case, he endorsed the government's charge while rejecting Microsoft's rebuttals.

He found that Microsoft had tried to divide the market for Internet browsing software with the Netscape Communications Corporation in 1995—a key charge in the government's case and a clearly illegal activity under antitrust law. He wrote that other companies had had similar encounters with Microsoft, and "these interactions demonstrate that it is Microsoft's corporate practice to pressure other firms to halt software development" that threatens Microsoft's dominance "or competes directly with Microsoft's most cherished software products."

He found that Microsoft's decision to bundle its Web browser with Windows and give it away free was not, as Microsoft asserted in court, simply an effort to add a desirable feature to Windows.

"Senior executives at Microsoft decided Microsoft needed to give its browser away in furtherance of the larger strategic goal of gaining market share," he wrote. Microsoft, he added, "viewed browser market share as the key to preserving its dominance."

And in one of his most damning findings, Judge Jackson concluded that "Web browsers and operating systems are separate products." Microsoft's key argument was that its browser was simply a feature of Windows, not a separate product.

He turned that argument around on Microsoft by finding that the company had actually harmed consumers by bundling the two products. Consumer harm is a key test in antitrust cases. Bundling the browser with Windows "unjustifiably jeopardized the stability and security of the operating system," meaning that he believed the government's argument that including the browser had made the operating system more likely to crash and more vulnerable to break-ins by intruders. "There is no technical justification for Microsoft's refusal to meet consumer demand for a browserless version of Windows 98," he added.

He wrote that Microsoft had threatened and bullied Apple Computer, Intel, America Online and other companies that Microsoft perceived as competitors. In the case of the International Business Machines Corporation, he wrote, "when IBM refused to abate the promotion of those of its own products that competed with Windows and Office," Microsoft's suite of business productivity software, "Microsoft punished the IBM PC Company with higher prices, a late license for Windows 95 and the withholding of technical and marketing support."

"Microsoft's past success in hurting such companies and stifling innovation deters investment in technologies and businesses that exhibit the potential to threaten Microsoft," the judge concluded. "The ultimate result is that some innovations that would truly benefit consumers never occur for the sole reason that they do not coincide with Microsoft's self interest."

Antitrust lawyers say they cannot recall another instance in which findings of fact in an antitrust case have been issued ahead of the actual verdict. "I've been at this for 40 years, and I've never heard of anything like this," said Stephen Axinn, an antitrust litigator at Axinn, Veltrop & Harkrider in New York.

Usually the findings are packaged with the conclusions of law—the legal precedents justifying a ruling—and the verdict. But Judge Jackson's decision to separate the findings offers at least two benefits.

"It's potentially a very clever thing to do," said Robert Litan, a former senior official in the Justice Department's antitrust division, now with the Brookings Institution.

For one thing, it will allow Judge Jackson to modify his final ruling if written responses from the litigants suggest to him that he might be standing on weak ground.

Publishing the findings ahead of the verdict also "prompts the parties to try to settle," said Andrew Gavil, a professor of law at Howard University. "This is a lot brighter than tea leaves. It tells the parties exactly where they stand."

Judge Jackson has repeatedly urged Microsoft and the government to settle the case.

"If it's progovernment, there's not much incentive for either side to settle," Litan said. "The government feels strong, and Microsoft waits—waits for the appeals court, or for another presidential administration" in just over a year. A new president will appoint a new head of the Justice Department's antitrust division, and Microsoft can hope that whoever that is will be inclined to settle on more generous terms.

Thomas Burt, a Microsoft lawyer, agreed with that analysis but added that Microsoft's leaders stand willing to discuss a settlement. Nevertheless, he said, they remain unified in their conviction that they will not accept any settlement that would jeopardize "our core value, the soul of our company, and that is the freedom to innovate and design products as we see fit."

The New York Times, November 6, 1999
http://www.nytimes.com/library/tech/99/11/biztech/articles/06soft.html

CRITICAL THINKING QUESTIONS

1. Explain why you agree or disagree with Judge Jackson's decision in the Microsoft case.
2. Explain why you believe Microsoft has grounds for appeal. Do you think the case should set precedence for dealing with technology-related antitrust issues?
3. Since technology seems to have changed the ways we communicate and do business, how can such transactions be monitored and controlled?
4. What position would you take in the Microsoft case if you were given the task to resolve the problem?

5. What, in your opinion, are the positive or negative aspects of regulation?
6. Why do you think the government should or should not function as a regulator of monopolies?
7. Explain the possible consequences of the quality of a product if a company is regulated.

STORY-SPECIFIC QUESTIONS

1. On what grounds did Judge Jackson determine that Microsoft was a monopoly?
2. What was the significance of Judge Jackson rendering a decision about the Microsoft case after the stock market closed?
3. How did the Justice Department react to the judge's decision? How did Microsoft react?

SHORT APPLICATION ASSIGNMENTS

1. In teams or individually, answer the story-specific questions; keep your answers to 25–75 words for each question.
2. In teams of three to five persons each, or as a whole class, discuss your responses to the critical thinking questions.
3. Prepare a one-page memo report (200–250 words) to your instructor in which you summarize this article. You will find a model one-page report on the Web site (nytimes.swcollege.com).
4. Write an executive summary (200–250 words). As an administrative assistant to a busy executive, you are expected to summarize selected articles and present important points. You will find a model executive summary on the Web site.
5. Summarize this article (100–125 words) for your company's newsletter. You will find a model newsletter on the Web site.

BUILDING RESEARCH SKILLS

1. Individually or in teams, use the Web to identify companies where antitrust regulation does or should apply. Your instructor may ask you to submit a three- to five-page essay, post a Web page or report your results in a five-minute presentation, along with a letter of transmittal explaining your essay.
2. Individually or in teams, defend or dispute the rights of Microsoft. Your instructor may ask you to submit a three- to five-page essay, post a Web page or report your results in a five-minute presentation, along with a letter of transmittal explaining your essay.
3. Using at least three other references (e.g., books, research-journal articles, newspaper or magazine stories or credible Web sites), write an 800- to 1,000-word essay that addresses two of the critical thinking questions offered earlier. Assume that your essay will be used as an internal reference for a government's policy guidelines.
4. Using at least three other references (e.g., books, research-journal articles, newspaper or magazine stories or credible Web sites), post an 800- to 1,000-word Web page that addresses at least two of the earlier critical thinking questions. Assume that your page will be posted in the policy section of a government's intranet.

As Welfare Benefits Expire, Second Thoughts

By Jason DeParle

Wisconsin, of all places, suddenly has the jitters about cutting families off welfare.

Since 1996, the state's famously tough work rules have swept more than 57,000 families from the rolls and turned a war on welfare into a social experiment commanding international attention. Almost 90 percent of the families that were getting welfare checks three years ago no longer receive them, and envious bureaucrats from around the globe visit the state to hear officials boast of the disappearing dole.

But Wisconsin is now grappling with the ultimate symbol of the new welfare age: time limits. Virtually everyone on welfare in the state is required to join a work program, and there are two-year limits on those jobs.

This month, for the first time, a handful of Wisconsin families have hit the deadline. As a result, they could lose their checks not for refusing to work for their aid, but simply for staying in the program too long.

The question of what to do with these families has everyone in the welfare system on edge, with the revealing exception of the poor themselves. In theory, time limits are supposed to push the needy down the path to self-reliance. In practice, most poor people are too tangled in the chaos of daily life to give them much thought. Instead, the limits have had an impact far more complex and indirect than the political slogans behind them.

What they have set into motion are waves of worry along bureaucratic fronts. Competing approaches to the deadlines' enforcement are in play as requests for extensions arrive.

The state officials who oversee the program are quarreling with the private agencies that help run it. And all are looking to avoid blame when families stay mired in problems that are sometimes decades in the making.

Amid the proliferating subplots, the deadlines have had at least one clearly positive effect: afraid of being called to task or even fined for their clients' slow progress, welfare agencies are revisiting old cases with new intensity.

But it remains unclear how much even the best social work can accomplish, especially as troubled lives compete with expiring clocks. And the heightened concern about these few families implicitly raises questions about the tens of thousands dropped from welfare before them without nearly as much thought.

Though the program, Wisconsin Works, or W-2, prides itself on being tough, so far the forces of caution have prevailed. Forty-eight recipients have sought extensions to the two-year limit and all have received them, putting off the day of reckoning by three to six months.

Among them was Robin Edwards, a 38-year-old mother of six who works as a janitor at a Milwaukee parochial school in exchange for a monthly welfare check of $673. A painfully shy woman who stares at the ground when she talks, she reads at the third-grade level and is unclear about such basics as what year her deadline expires. "I'm really not too sure," she said.

In fact, her time expired this month. As it did, it added to the concern up the bureaucratic ladder.

At Y-W Works, a private agency in Milwaukee that handles her case, social workers redoubled a two-year effort to help Ms. Edwards find a regular wage-paying job. Sabrina Lee returned to Ms. Edwards's problems with child care. Pepita Johnson gave weekly lessons on talking to employers. Mark Miller lined up interviews at a hospital and a grocery.

The challenges before them were considerable. In the past 10 years, Ms. Edwards had held just one private job, for a few weeks. Among the skills she is trying to acquire are the rudiments of workplace grooming. "They tell me, 'Don't go in there with body odor on you,' " she said.

As the social workers attended to Ms. Edwards, the head of Y-W Works, Julia Taylor, asked the state for more time.

J. Jean Rogers, the state official who oversees W-2, personally sifted through two years of case notes to review the agency's work.

Ms. Rogers, a strict critic of welfare, gave Ms. Edwards three more months, but only after urging Y-W Works to follow a seven-point plan.

"Contact employers with whom she has interviewed to determine for certain why she is not being hired," she wrote. "Engage her in family planning." Ms. Rogers's decisions, in turn, are reviewed by aides to her boss, Linda Stewart, the Secretary of the Department of Workforce Development, who is considered more of a moderate.

The entire process is buffeted by competing political concerns. Saying many families have not received enough help, critics of W-2 have threatened to sue on behalf of the first recipients who lose their aid.

"The state should extend the deadline for everyone, given the disarray the program was in," said Pat DeLessio, a welfare rights lawyer.

But others are warning against retreat. "We have to make sure that time limits have teeth," said State Representative John Gard, a Republican who sponsored the legislation creating W-2. If extensions become the rule, he said, "we'll need to scrutinize this closely."

As for Ms. Edwards, though she is getting a remarkable amount of attention, her circumstances are not particularly remarkable. Officials often describe the last cases as the hardest, but that is not necessarily so. Work programs like W-2 sometimes affect the most troubled families first: addicted, depressed or disturbed clients often just disappear. For every client now getting a second look, there may well be two or three others with similar problems who vanished into the post-welfare world.

Ms. Edwards herself had a spotty history in the program, sometimes missing weeks of work. But Y-W Works continued to pursue her. And its efforts just produced a result that took her by surprise: She got a job. On October 1 she began working three days a week as a janitor at a Toys 'R' Us.

No one pretends her problems are solved. With only a part-time job, Ms. Edwards is still on welfare—she now sweeps the school two days a week—and her clock is still ticking. Supporters of time limits would call her breakthrough a testament to the power of deadlines. Critics would describe her as a vulnerable woman whose safety net is shrinking.

Her supervisor at the school, Venus McMurry, sounds a pessimistic note. "I don't care what anybody says, the girl's not ready to work," Ms. McMurry said.

Ms. Edwards offers no predictions about where this experiment is heading. "Hopefully, I'll have some luck," she said.

THE COUNTRY: CLINTON'S PROPOSAL SEIZED BY REPUBLICANS

Though they swept the country appearing inevitable, time limits on welfare were anything but. Until Bill Clinton ran for President in 1992, few welfare experts had pondered them and no states had tried them.

Although time limits are now hailed by conservatives, they were first proposed by a liberal, Professor David T. Ellwood, an economist at Harvard.

He wanted to give the poor two or three years of training and then require those still on the rolls to work for their checks. But they would remain eligible for aid, with the Government providing the jobs, if necessary, along with other services.

President Clinton used that plan as a template for his 1992 pledge to "end welfare as we know it." Like Professor Ellwood, Clinton merely proposed sending the poor to a work site after a few years. He never suggested dropping them from the rolls.

But conservatives seized on his bold rhetoric and called for doing just that. "Ending welfare," they argued, meant enforcing finite periods of eligibility, period. Otherwise, they said, the poor would lack the motivation to leave welfare.

Soon, this new definition prevailed: not time limits followed by work assignments, but time limits followed by nothing. Under attack for failing to keep his "end welfare" pledge, President Clinton accepted a Republican plan in 1996, signing a law that placed a five-year lifetime limit on eligibility for Federal benefits.

The law permits states to set shorter limits, and Wisconsin is one of 20 to do so. It also allows states to exempt 20 percent of their welfare families from the deadline. Wisconsin has no outright exemptions, though there is no limit on the number of extensions a recipient can seek.

At first, time limits appeared to be one of the most consequential features of the new welfare law. The Urban Institute, a Washington research group, predicted that of the 5 million families then on welfare, 1.4 million would suddenly be dropped in 2001 when their five-year limit expired.

But a good economy and tough work rules have already cut the country's welfare rolls nearly in half, and as a result, the impact that time limits will come to have is now less clear. Many of the 2.7 million families still receiving aid are expected to leave the rolls before their deadlines expire.

And after such precipitous reductions, states may approach the deadlines more permissively than once expected.

So far, the state evidence is mixed. Some of the largest have rejected the strict limits envisioned by Federal law. California and New York, which account for a third of the nation's recipients, have said that after five years they will reduce, but not eliminate, a family's cash aid.

If necessary, they will finance the continued payments themselves.

Massachusetts, by contrast, is rigorously enforcing a two-year limit.

Of the first 5,000 families to reach the limit, about 70 percent lost their cash assistance. (Time limits do not affect food stamps or Medicaid.) Similarly, Louisiana dropped 4,200 families this year, about 10 percent of its caseload, after they reached a two-year limit. Time limits in Connecticut have cut the most families, about 19,000, but the vast majority were working families who would have been ineligible for welfare in most states.

For evidence about how the limits work, most analysts turn to Pensacola, Florida, which began experimenting with them in 1994. As in Wisconsin, the poor seemed to pay the deadlines little mind. Families given limits of two or three years left the rolls no quicker than a control group of other families.

But researchers found that the Pensacola program, like Wisconsin's, did motivate caseworkers. "They felt like they really had to pay attention to people as they approached the time limit," said Dan Bloom of the Manpower Demonstration Research Corporation, a New York City group that evaluated the program.

Likening time limits to shock therapy, Bloom said creative managers might be able to find other ways to motivate caseworkers. But, he added, "it's harder."

THE STATE: CONFLICTING VISIONS ABOUT TIME LIMITS

Wisconsin would seem the last place to fret about families losing welfare. When Governor Tommy G. Thompson, a Republican, took office in 1987 after an anti-welfare campaign, there were nearly 100,000 families on the rolls. Now there are 7,700.

But as a few dozen families now seek extensions, tensions are running high. Consider the jousting around Simona Alva, a Mexican immigrant who went on welfare seven years ago after her husband fell ill with epileptic seizures.

An outgoing woman with 11 children and 10 cockatiels, Ms. Alva insists that her ability to work is limited. She speaks no English. She gets lost on city buses. Though seven of her children are grown, she worries that a mentally ill son, who is 24, will burn down the house without her supervision.

And like many Hispanic women, who are leaving welfare more slowly than blacks or whites, she feels her place is in her home, watching over her troubled family.

"The woman is supposed to take care of the man," she said.

Since joining W-2, Ms. Alva has held the least demanding of two major types of jobs in the program, called a "transitions" job. She spends four hours a day, under close supervision, packing books and calendars. But with eligibility at each job level limited to two years, she is now expected to move up to a more demanding "community service" job, with longer hours, or leave welfare.

The combined eligibility for all work levels is five years. Because clients are generally required to move up the ladder, those who start in community service, as most do, are typically expected to leave the program for regular jobs after two years. They are the ones most affected by the current deadline.

In Ms. Alva's case, Y-W Works, the private agency, requested an extension, arguing that her ability to work is "complicated by her husband's and her son's disabilities." State officials were skeptical. "This seems to be a person who is ready to move up," they wrote.

The agency resisted. ("Her illiteracy renders her vulnerable in the workplace.") The state pushed back. ("She can communicate functionally.") In the end, the state gave Ms. Alva six more months to study English and to find care for her husband and son.

These first decisions have been shaped by at least three layers of bureaucratic politics. One involves tensions between the private welfare agencies and advocacy groups for the poor.

Eager to avoid a lawsuit, some agencies are seeking extensions for any client who wants one, shifting the burden to the state. "It's a game of chicken to see who's going to be the first to make a denial," said an official at one agency.

To circumvent the limits, some agencies are also quietly shifting clients to an easier level of work—buying them two more years of eligibility. As the deadlines approached, the number of Milwaukee clients placed in the least-taxing "transitions" jobs grew 11 percent as the overall rolls declined.

A second level of tension pits the agencies against the state. Under state contract, agencies can be fined $5,000 for any "failure to serve" a client. So far, no fines have been issued, but Ms. Rogers, the presiding state official, has sometimes criticized the Milwaukee agencies. With Ms. Rogers examining every request for an extension herself, a flurry of social work is sometimes intended as a defense. A third level of tension exists among state officials, as suggested by the contrasting tenor of their remarks in recent interviews.

Ms. Rogers is a firm believer in time limits who has longtime ties to the Governor. "If time limits are serious, you have to treat them seriously," she said. "You don't just look for some external reason" for extensions. Her boss, Ms. Stewart, sounded less stern.

"I don't think our legislators expect us to be punitive toward people," she said.

THE AGENCY: LIMITS PRODUCE MORE SOCIAL WORK

Amid the tensions, families that might have been left to languish are getting a second look. At Y-W Works, a weekly brainstorming session shows the personalized attention that the system can muster at its best. Client by client, a roomful of social workers revisited the struggles of people approaching the deadline.

Here is one: "She's a schizophrenic who refuses to take her medication."

And another: "She finds it hard to stop using marijuana."

And another: "She just plain flat out doesn't have the emotional energy to do anything about where she is in life."

While such personal attention was missing from the old welfare system, its achievements remain unclear.

Teams of workers were sent to the homes of the schizophrenic woman and the woman on marijuana. But that was just a start. The depressed woman had the group stumped. Her Medicaid plan will pay for only six visits with a therapist. "We've got to find something better than that," her caseworker said.

If the meeting shows the system at its most conscientious, it also shows that clients can—indeed, often do—still fall through the cracks. After all, these are families who have made little progress in nearly two years.

Sometimes caseworkers miss problems. Often clients hide problems.

Turnover among caseworkers is high. And families that move must often start at a new agency, as cases are apportioned geographically. The schizophrenic woman, for instance, had had been seen by three other agencies.

While Ms. DeLessio, the welfare rights lawyer, called Y-W Works one of the more attentive agencies, she said the system as a whole had failed to live up to the promises behind time limits. "The whole idea is we were going to do these individualized assessments and get people the services they need," she said. "That did not happen."

Ms. Taylor, the agency head, says the issue is less the casework than the difficulty of the cases. Of the first 10 Y-W Works clients to reach their limit, 5 were physically disabled or caring for disabled relatives. Five spoke little or no English. On average, they had a fifth-grade reading level and had been on welfare for the last seven years.

Time limits "do help create a sense of urgency, and sometimes that's helpful," Ms. Taylor said. "But we're dealing with really difficult problems. It's not something that's going to necessarily get solved in two years."

In mulling extensions, sometimes the hardest cases are easiest, because the need for more time seems most obvious. Such is the case with Elise Moore, another schizophrenic woman. She often refuses medication and will attend her work assignment only if her housemate comes with her. Even then, she often flees.

"If I hear voices, I'm gone," she says. "I don't want to be around people when I start to scream."

Her case generated no dissent: state officials quickly agreed to an additional six months. Y-W Works plans to use the time to help Ms. Moore reapply for Federal disability benefits.

A more difficult challenge, in Wisconsin and beyond, involves people with less obvious but perhaps no less disabling, problems. On the surface, Loretta Triplett, 48, seems, if anything, overdue to leave welfare for work. She has a high school diploma. Three of her four children are grown.

And she insists she could find work if she had to. "It needs to be a position I'm going to enjoy," she said.

In a program that promotes entry-level work, statements like that, if taken alone, could disqualify her from an extension.

But inside, Ms. Triplett is stalked by more than finicky standards. She has battled depression for 35 years and tried medication without success. Tensions at home add to her worries. She says her son drinks heavily, and with her daughter susceptible to depression, Ms. Triplett must often care for three young grandchildren. She is self-conscious about her missing front teeth, and she conducts job interviews—indeed, most conversations—through clenched lips. "I don't like to smile," she said.

Tight-lipped about her problems as well, Ms. Triplett began opening up to a counselor at Y-W Works only recently, shortly before her benefits were scheduled to expire.

If they do, she will join legions of Wisconsin women in the post-welfare world, many with similar problems. About two-thirds find at least sporadic work, according to most surveys. Others turn to family or boyfriends. Relatively few have wound up on the streets. But relatively few have escaped poverty. Most simply find new ways to get by. Ms. Triplett said that if she lost welfare she would move in with her mother.

In June, Ms. Triplett began a new work assignment, at the electric company. Arguing she could gain new clerical skills, Y-W Works asked for another six months. The state gave her three.

"We don't want to cut her off," said Anne Paczesny, her counselor. "We see her as making progress. It's just not as fast as W-2 wants."

The New York Times, October 10, 1999
http://www.nytimes.com/library/national/101099wis-welfare.html

CRITICAL THINKING QUESTIONS

1. Should time limits be applied in welfare reform programs? Why, or why not?
2. Has Wisconsin successfully taken care of its needy citizens by instituting this program? Why, or why not?
3. Discuss ways in which caseworkers can do a better job of preparing welfare recipients for the workforce.
4. What are the costs and benefits of welfare reform programs such as the one in Wisconsin?

STORY-SPECIFIC QUESTIONS

1. Why were time limits established in the Wisconsin Works program?
2. Describe the assistance W-2 clients get from Y-W Works.
3. Summarize the elements of Clinton's welfare reform plan.

SHORT APPLICATION ASSIGNMENTS

1. In teams or individually, answer the story-specific questions; keep your answers to 25–75 words for each question.
2. In teams of three to five persons each, or as a whole class, discuss your responses to the critical thinking questions.
3. Prepare a one-page memo report (200–250 words) to your instructor in which you summarize this article. You will find a model one-page report on the Web site (nytimes.swcollege.com).
4. Write an executive summary (200–250 words). As an administrative assistant to a busy executive, you are expected to summarize selected articles and present important points. You will find a model executive summary on the Web site.
5. Summarize this article (100–125 words) for your company's newsletter. You will find a model newsletter on the Web site.

BUILDING RESEARCH SKILLS

1. Individually or in teams, analyze other states' welfare reform programs. How are they similar to and different from Wisconsin's program? Your instructor may ask you to submit a three- to five-page essay, post a Web page or report your results in a five-minute presentation, along with a letter of transmittal explaining your essay.
2. Using at least three other references (e.g., books, research-journal articles, newspaper or magazine stories or credible Web sites), write an 800- to 1,000-word essay that addresses two of the critical thinking questions offered earlier. Assume that your essay will be used as an internal reference for a government's policy guidelines.
3. Using at least three other references (e.g., books, research-journal articles, newspaper or magazine stories or credible Web sites), post an 800- to 1,000-word Web page that addresses at least two of the earlier critical thinking questions. Assume that your page will be posted in the policy section of a government's intranet.

CHAPTER 4

Personal Economics

PREVIEW

Many view material wealth and large incomes as symbolic of America's economic progress. Moreover, the federal government uses income and related information to identify the range of prosperity and poverty in the country. However, recent studies show that more people are losing ground in the quest for a desirable standard of living. In fact, there has been a dramatic decline in the income of the poor, while the rich seem to be getting richer. And this growing income gap affects people of all ages, including retirees.

Today, the chance that a family will experience poverty has increased considerably. Despite more than three decades of government-sponsored, anti-poverty programs and efforts to "retrain" workers for the changing workplace, the disparities between the rich and poor appear to be more pronounced. David Cay Johnston examines how the distance between rich and poor is a national concern, in his article "Gap Between Rich and Poor Found Substantially Wider."

And as Mr. Johnston explains in another article, "A Growing Gap Between the Savers and the Save-Nots," the income gap often follows individuals into their retirement. Governmental concerns about retirement, as illustrated in Barbara Crosette's "Great Expectations: The Retirement Mentality vs. Reality," go beyond income gaps and will keep economists busy well into the twenty-first century.

Source: Christine M. Thompson/CyberTimes

49

Gap Between Rich and Poor Found Substantially Wider

By David Cay Johnston

The gap between rich and poor has grown into an economic chasm so wide that this year the richest 2.7 million Americans, the top 1 percent, will have as many after-tax dollars to spend as the bottom 100 million.

That ratio has more than doubled since 1977, when the top 1 percent had as much as the bottom 49 million, according to new data from the Congressional Budget Office.

In dollars, the richest 2.7 million people and the 100 million at the other end of the scale will each have about $620 billion to spend, according to an analysis of the budget office figures.

The analysis was done by the Center on Budget and Policy Priorities, a nonprofit organization in Washington that advocates Federal tax and spending policies that it says would benefit the poor.

The analysis, released last night, seems certain to stoke the debate that is about to resume in Washington over projected Federal budget surpluses and possible tax cuts.

The data from the budget office show that income disparity has grown so much that four out of five households, or about 217 million people, are taking home a thinner slice of the economic pie today than in 1977.

When adjusted for inflation, as all of the income figures have been, these households' share of national income has fallen to just under 50 percent from 56 percent in 1977.

But among the most prosperous one-fifth of Americans households, or about 54 million people, whose share of the national income grew, that fatter slice of the pie was not sliced evenly. More than 90 percent of the increase is going to the richest 1 percent of households, which this year will average $515,600 in after-tax income, up from $234,700 in 1977.

Since 1993, the economy has lifted the incomes of all of the income groups tracked by the budget office, but the incomes of the richest Americans are rising twice as fast as those of the middle class. In addition, the budget office figures understate the economic power of the richest 1 percent because they exclude deferred forms of income like restricted stock, which have grown rapidly in recent years as companies have expanded their pay plans from senior executives down to store and plant manager levels.

Though the economic pie has grown over the past 22 years, the Congressional Budget Office data show that the poorest one-fifth of households have not shared in this bounty. The average after-tax household income of the poor, adjusted for inflation, has fallen 12 percent since 1977. So the poor not only have a small slice of a big economic pie, but the pie is bigger and their piece is even smaller.

The poorest one-fifth of households will average $8,800 of income this year, down from $10,000 in 1977.

Congressional Republicans have passed legislation to cut taxes by $792 billion over the next 10 years, legislation that President Clinton has promised to veto, saying it is imprudent and favors the rich.

The Republicans say that a tax cut is justified because Federal tax revenue rose last year to 21.7 percent of the economy, the highest since World War II, and because the Congressional Budget Office anticipates surpluses as far into the future as its projections go.

The Republicans acknowledge that most of their proposed tax cuts will go to taxpayers making $100,000 or more a year, but they say that since these high-income Americans pay 62 percent of Federal income taxes they should get most of the benefits of a tax cut.

"The tax bill's benefits are roughly proportional to the taxes that each taxpayer pays," Bruce Bartlett, a Treasury official in the Reagan and Bush Administrations, has written.

President Clinton, who says that budget surpluses may never materialize, wants to pay down the national debt before cutting taxes. He also says that a tax cut should not bestow the bulk of its benefits on the rich, and he wants part of any surplus to finance new programs.

The budget and policy center's report says that one reason the rich are doing so well is the cumulative effect of tax cuts since 1977, when the top Federal income tax bracket was 50 percent, compared with the current 39.6 percent.

These tax cuts are worth an average of $40,000 this year to each of the slightly more than one million households that make up the top 1 percent, said Robert Greenstein, executive director of the Center on Budget and Policy Priorities.

Internal Revenue Service tax return data, not cited in the center's report, show that two-thirds of Americans earned less than $40,000 in 1997.

"Many Americans who make $80,000 a year, $100,000 or $120,000, think of themselves as middle class," Greenstein said, "but the fact is that while these people are not rich, they are also not in or even near the middle, which is only about $32,000 in after-tax income."

Greenstein said that under the Republican tax cut plan the richest 1 percent of households would save an average of $32,000 more annually, once all of the proposed cuts were phased in.

The budget and policy center has been sharply critical of the Republican tax cut plan and the idea that those who pay the most in taxes should get the biggest cuts.

Isaac Shapiro, who wrote the report with Greenstein, called the proposed tax cut plan "wrongheaded" and unfair to both the poor and the middle class.

Greenstein said he was pleased with one proposal in the Republican plan, a small expansion of the Earned Income Tax Credit, which allows low-income workers to collect up to $3,816 this year in refunds of their Social Security tax and a cash payment that is a form of negative income tax.

A couple with two children does not pay any income tax until their income exceeds $28,000 this year.

That expansion was proposed despite intense criticism of the credit by leading Republicans, notably Representative Bill Archer, Republican of Texas and the chairman of the House Ways and Means Committee.

Other data, not cited in the budget and policy center report, also show that the growth in incomes is mostly at the top of the income ladder.

For example, 142,566 Americans reported $1 million or more of adjusted gross income for 1997, nearly two-thirds more than the 86,998 such taxpayers in 1995.

Frank Levy, an economist at the Massachusetts Institute of Technology whose review of two books taking different tacks on the income gap appears in the current issue of the *Harvard Business Review*, said that the concentration of income growth at the top resulted largely from rules set by Congress.

"Markets are obviously very important in the economy," Professor Levy said, "but they are surrounded by a lot of rules—rules about how easy it is to organize unions and how free trade is—and those rules are determined by the political process and those rules right now are shaped by money" donated to political candidates.

The New York Times, September 5, 1999
http://www.nytimes.com/library/national/090599gap-rich-poor.html

CRITICAL THINKING QUESTIONS

1. What circumstances or conditions (political, social or economic) have contributed to the widening gap between the rich and the poor? How have they contributed?
2. Explain the effects, if any, that a tax cut would have on reducing the number of low income people in this country.
3. Do you think the earned income tax credit is a good idea? Why, or why not?

STORY-SPECIFIC QUESTIONS

1. How large is the gap between rich and poor in this country as addressed in this article?
2. Why did Republicans believe a tax cut was justified?
3. How did the Center on Budget and Policy Priorities respond to the proposed tax cut?

SHORT APPLICATION ASSIGNMENTS

1. In teams or individually, answer the story-specific questions; keep your answers to 25–75 words for each question.
2. In teams of three to five persons each, or as a whole class, discuss your responses to the critical thinking questions.
3. Prepare a one-page memo report (200–250 words) to your instructor in which you summarize this article. You will find a model one-page report on the Web site (nytimes.swcollege.com).
4. Write an executive summary (200–250 words). As an administrative assistant to a busy executive, you are expected to summarize selected articles and present important points. You will find a model executive summary on the Web site.
5. Summarize this article (100–125 words) for your company's newsletter. You will find a model newsletter on the Web site.

BUILDING RESEARCH SKILLS

1. Individually or in teams, investigate the current gap between the rich and poor in the United States. How has this changed over the last few decades? Why has this changed? Your instructor may ask you to submit a three- to five-page essay, post a Web page or report your results in a five-minute presentation, along with a letter of transmittal explaining your essay.
2. Individually or in teams, investigate the current gap between the rich and poor in a foreign country. How does this compare to the gap in the United States? How has this changed over the last few decades? Why has this changed? Your instructor may ask you to submit a three- to five-page essay, post a Web page or report your results in a five-minute presentation, along with a letter of transmittal explaining your essay.
3. Using at least three other references (e.g., books, research-journal articles, newspaper or magazine stories or credible Web sites), write an 800- to 1,000-word essay that addresses two of the critical thinking questions offered earlier. Assume that your essay will be used as an internal reference for a government's policy guidelines.
4. Using at least three other references (e.g., books, research-journal articles, newspaper or magazine stories or credible Web sites), post an 800- to 1,000-word Web page that addresses at least two of the earlier critical thinking questions. Assume that your page will be posted in the policy section of a government's intranet.

A Growing Gap Between
the Savers and the Save-Nots

By David Cay Johnston

In two years, when the first of the baby boomers turn 55 and become eligible for early retirement, a new trend should begin to emerge that will separate the ants from the grasshoppers.

And two decades from now, when half the boomers will have ended their working years, that trend will have grown into a major economic divide, one much bigger than the current split between the few at the top with rising incomes and the many struggling from paycheck to paycheck.

The great divide will be wealth. Wealth is not income. Indeed, some people with modest incomes are prodigious savers, while many high-income people save little or nothing.

Wealth will affect how long boomers live (the better off people are, the greater their life expectancy) and how happy they are in retirement, although the relationship between wealth and happiness in retirement is not simple, the few experts who have studied the issue say.

For four decades much of the national debate about economic well-being has focused on incomes and, especially, on their growing disparity: Nearly all real growth has gone to the top 5 percent of workers, while those at the bottom have lost ground.

But now that debate is encompassing wealth. The Ford Foundation, whose grants have had enormous influence on policies affecting the poor, has begun steering academic and Government attention to helping the poor not just by raising their incomes, but by helping them acquire assets, especially savings accounts and homes.

And the disparity in wealth is far greater than in incomes. Four out of five working-age Americans essentially have no wealth, except for equity in their homes, while in 1997 the top 1 percent owned 48.6 percent of all financial assets like stocks and bonds. That is the greatest concentration in the nation's history, said Professor Edward N. Wolff, a New York University economist who studies wealth.

The most important division among today's retirees is between those who own their own homes and those who don't: homeowners retire with an average net worth of $115,000, while nonhomeowners have $800.

In the years ahead this gap will grow. The ants, the thrifty boomers who have saved and invested, will have plenty of money to spend. Some ants will be able to spend twice as much in retirement as they did in their working years, said Jonathan Skinner, a Dartmouth College economist who studies retirement savings.

But the much bigger group is the grasshoppers, who spend what they earn, whether it is a little or a lot, and are slaves to minimum monthly payments on their plastic debt, have 125 percent mortgages on their homes and who, when they change jobs, dip into their 401(k) savings.

The differences between the current crop of retired ants and grasshoppers are masked by traditional, or defined benefit, pension plans, which guarantee a monthly check for life. Combined with Social Security and home ownership, such pensions have changed retirement in America from a time of widespread poverty four decades ago to an era of comfort for many and golden years for more than a few.

Social Security and Medicare, that other pillar of retirement, are, of course, at the heart of a huge Washington debate. But despite all that well-publicized uncertainty, the baby boomers who start retiring will find the rest of their lives shaped by a change that happened with next to no public discussion: the switch from traditional pensions.

Far fewer boomers have such check-a-month plans than do retirees today. Many of them have changed jobs so often that their pensions will replace only a tiny slice of the incomes in their working years, because these plans bestow most of their benefits on people who stay with one company for their entire career.

Instead, the boomers are much more likely to rely on 401(k) savings plans and other so-called defined contribution plans in which they assume all or most of the risks of investing.

Overly conservative investment choices, too much ownership of employer stock and the fact that 84 percent of people dip into their 401(k) plans each time they change jobs means that in the new world of retirement plans, many boomers will retire with too few resources to live the retirement life they want.

Of course, this system will also produce a few big winners among people who saved a lot or bought stocks that exploded in value.

How much will this matter? Lacking a crystal ball, the best indicator of what this will mean to future retirees is the insight scholars have gained into how money affects the happiness of people nearing retirement and those already retired.

The first finding is that people generally do just fine with less. Most people experience a sharp drop in spendable income when they retire, and most adapt quickly and easily, said Sylvester J. Schieber, the research director for Watson Wyatt Worldwide, a compensation consulting company, and a noted authority on pensions and Social Security.

In general, retirees do well if pensions, Social Security and savings replace 60 percent to 70 percent of their job earnings, percentages that Schieber said may be a bit higher than what people need simply to feel comfortable.

Problems arise when the drop in income is more severe, especially if it plunges a person down the social ladder.

According to Professor Skinner of Dartmouth, "There are a bunch of people who have done pretty well in terms of getting ready for retirement, some because of good pension coverage and some because of wealth."

But there is a large group of people—perhaps 20 percent—who seem to be walking into a brick wall at retirement, he said, discovering that their resources are woefully inadequate.

Ultimately, Professor Skinner said, how well-off people are in retirement is not an economic issue, but one of well-being and contentment.

"We don't know a lot about these issues," he said, "except that severely ratcheting consumption downward leads to stress and that people who don't save much die earlier."

Professor George Lowenstein of Carnegie Mellon University, who is an economist and a psychologist, is one of the few scholars who have looked at how retirement income affects happiness.

Professor Lowenstein found that white-collar workers in low-status jobs enjoyed retirement more than either high-status white-collar workers or blue-collar workers. And he found that except for people who found themselves plunged into poverty, or into an income level so far below their working lifestyle that their social status changed, most people are happy in retirement.

His surveys also found that people worry more about having enough to retire in the five years before they stop working than after they quit.

"The financial press and the mutual fund industry are telling people that you need to save a lot, that you should be worried, and people work themselves into a state of anxiety," Professor Lowenstein said. "But even though income drops after retirement and consumption drops even more, people find it is not nearly as bad as they expected. People adapt to adverse circumstances much faster than they expect."

He added: "The amount of misery they experience worrying about whether they have enough to retire is far out of proportion to the misery people actually experience after they retire."

Curiously, he observed, surveys show that people who have accumulated assets worry more about not having enough than do those with few assets. In that way, the shift from traditional pensions to owning assets and having to manage them is taking a psychological toll.

The least happy retirees, Professor Lowenstein said, are those forced into retirement because of layoffs or poor health. Indeed, poor health is by far the number one factor cited among unhappy retirees. Baby boomers are expected on average to live a bit more than 17 years after reaching age 65, with those with more money enjoying better health and longer lives because of generally better medical care and diet and more healthful lifestyles.

Facts like that reinforce economists' tendency to equate greater wealth with greater happiness, Professor Lowenstein said, but a review of surveys from around the world shows such a relationship is weak.

A great divide may be coming, but he believes only those grasshoppers who have lived well and saved nothing so that their circumstances change drastically for the worse are likely to experience much psychological pain in retirement.

"Almost all the research," he said, "points to the conclusion that retired people, for the most part, are happy and satisfied with their lives to a degree that they had not anticipated prior to retirement."

The New York Times, March 21, 1999
http://www.nytimes.com/library/financial/sunday/032199retire-johnston.html

CRITICAL THINKING QUESTIONS

1. What do you think about instituting a mandatory national "savings" program that would supplement social security and pension programs?
2. Why do you think some people do not have good savings habits?
3. Why do you think people with substantial wealth and assumed financial security worry more about accumulating more assets than those without such assets?
4. Do you think the rich should be obliged to provide assistance to poor people through taxation? Why, or why not?

STORY-SPECIFIC QUESTIONS

1. What has been the recent goal of the Ford Foundation regarding helping the poor?
2. What financial habits distinguish ants from grasshoppers?
3. What will baby boomers most likely use as an alternative to the traditional pension plan?

SHORT APPLICATION ASSIGNMENTS

1. In teams or individually, answer the story-specific questions; keep your answers to 25–75 words for each question.
2. In teams of three to five persons each, or as a whole class, discuss your responses to the critical thinking questions.
3. Prepare a one-page memo report (200–250 words) to your instructor in which you summarize this article. You will find a model one-page report on the Web site (nytimes.swcollege.com).
4. Write an executive summary (200–250 words). As an administrative assistant to a busy executive, you are expected to summarize selected articles and present important points. You will find a model executive summary on the Web site.
5. Summarize this article (100–125 words) for your company's newsletter. You will find a model newsletter on the Web site.

BUILDING RESEARCH SKILLS

1. Individually or in teams, review the U.S. (http://www.fedstats.gov/) and other related resources (http://stats.bls.gov/oreother.htm) that provide statistical details about U.S. consumer and spending habits. Identify the areas where most consumers allocate their income. Your instructor may ask you to submit a three- to five-page essay, post a Web page or report your results in a five-minute presentation, along with a letter of transmittal explaining your essay.

2. Individually or in teams, review consumer and spending habits of another country (http://stats.bls.gov/oreother.htm). Identify the areas where most consumers allocate their income. How does this compare to the United States? Your instructor may ask you to submit a three- to five-page essay, post a Web page or report your results in a five-minute presentation, along with a letter of transmittal explaining your essay.

3. Using at least three other references (e.g., books, research-journal articles, newspaper or magazine stories or credible Web sites), write an 800- to 1,000-word essay that addresses two of the critical thinking questions offered earlier. Assume that your essay will be used as an internal reference for a government's policy guidelines.

4. Using at least three other references (e.g., books, research-journal articles, newspaper or magazine stories or credible Web sites), post an 800- to 1,000-word Web page that addresses at least two of the earlier critical thinking questions. Assume that your page will be posted in the policy section of a government's intranet.

Great Expectations: The Retirement Mentality vs. Reality

By Barbara Crosette

United Nations—The United States is far from alone when it comes to worrying about how to sustain a long-term Social Security system in an era of aging populations—or how to insure that there will be enough new talent to fill the workplace as fewer babies are born and more people retire. Around the world, but particularly in Europe and richer Asian nations, the situation is even more alarming, and so are the choices governments may soon have to make.

Persuading people to retire later may seem like the easiest alternative, but planners worldwide are finding that cultural and social attitudes toward leisure, family, old age and status have a great effect on policymaking. Along with economic globalization and urbanization, the idea of a hard-earned, dignified and pleasurable retirement is catching on in many countries.

"Within the space of about 100 years, people have not only accepted, but grown to believe that retirement is a right somehow, a human right almost," said Dalmer Hoskins, secretary general of the International Social Security Association in Geneva. "Working with these 150 countries that have pensions system, I'm struck more by the commonalities among them than the differences."

No one knows exactly what a decent level of retirement living is, he said, "but it's written into the constitutions of country after country."

The question, as Mr. Hoskins frames it, is whether more retirement is really what most economies really need, particularly in industrialized Europe, where populations are shrinking and aging, and most people are retiring before the age of 60 and living another 20 years or more. He suggests that in Europe and the United States, national interests and those of private enterprise may be dangerously out of sync.

"The private sector is retiring people at consistently earlier ages," he said, adding that forcing people to retire in the name of downsizing and reorganization has gone hand in hand with the shirking of responsibility for pension plans.

Big, even cosmic, ideas float around the subject of retirement. Peter G. Peterson, an investment banker and chairman of the Institute for International Economics, argued in *Gray Dawn: How the Coming Age Wave Will Transform America—and the World* (Times Books, 1999) that, "We are confronting demographic changes so substantive that they could redefine economic and political systems in the developed countries over the next generation." Early retirement, he asserted, is already undermining the survival of developed nations.

Unless people can be persuaded to work longer into old age, say Mr. Peterson and others, like Joseph Chamie, director of the United Nations Population Division, developed countries will have to accept a loss of productivity, creativity and even general economic health.

Or they will be forced to accept waves of immigration from poorer nations, a policy Germany, other European countries and Japan would like to avoid for social and cultural reasons.

In the United States, one serious hurdle is ageism, Mr. Peterson says, reflecting on the youth culture that pervades many American companies. "Overcoming ageism will requiring ongoing education and commitment, much as overcoming racism in American workplaces has over the past few years," he writes. "An entire stereotype will have to be reversed, along with all the institutional rules and habits of thought that perpetuate it."

Don't bother, a lot of retirees seem to be saying, as they settle into country club retirement communities or book another cruise.

In Singapore, where the proportion of people 60 or older will rise to 26 percent from the current 10 percent in the next 30 years, the Government hopes to push the retirement age from 62 to 67. But Singaporeans, who must contribute to a national savings plan, can take their accumulated retirement package at age 55, and a fair number do, said Dr. Kanwal Jit Soin, a former independent member of Parliament.

"People think they deserve retirement by the age of 55 or 60," she said in an interview, adding that this is particularly true of older people with few or no professional qualifications or skills, born before Singapore's economy took off. "And we are also a society with strong filial ideals," said Dr. Soin, an orthopedic surgeon. "Children take care of their parents and grandparents look after their grandchildren."

With Singapore's standard of living now rivaling southern Europe's, retirees also go on cruises and vacations that they could never have afforded in earlier decades.

Singapore—with a dominant Chinese population but a mix of people of Indian, Malay and European ancestry—is almost alone among Asian nations in changing its immigration policy to allow more foreigners with skills to settle in the small country, really an island city-state. It also allows unskilled workers, most from poorer Asian nations, to work for limited periods, filling manual jobs that Singapore's 3.5 million people have largely outgrown through education and training for a technological future.

Japan takes a different approach, rejecting increased immigration. It tries to keep people working longer through incentives to their employers, said Linda G. Martin, president of the Population Council in New York.

"The Japanese Government has a fairly aggressive policy to encourage employers to retain older workers," she said. "It provides some financial incentives to companies that maintain a certain percentage of older employees, and sometimes older workers retire and are rehired by the same company, often with a lesser title or lower stature.

"The Japanese," she added, "are a bit ahead of the United States in how to make productive use of older people."

In the third world, where most people keep on working to survive, the formal retirement situation is very mixed, and sometimes more complicated. A survey of retirement ages by the United Nations Population Division shows the lowest ages in the poorest countries, mostly African, but also several in South Asia. Yet these are also often places where there are no pensions or other benefits, no social security systems and no subsidized health plans. A low national retirement age—the lowest is 40 in the Solomon Islands—often reflects short life expectancy, the pressure of younger working-age populations, or both.

In India, the employed are squeezed from both ends of the age scale, with millions of young people joining the workforce every year, while older people are living longer than ever before and are beginning to demand retirement programs. Since independence in 1947, India has raised life expectancy to 63 from 39. But until very recently it retained a 58-year-old mandatory retirement age for Government employees, opening places for younger people but forcing even experienced ambassadors and key civil servants to search for work. The age has now been raised to 60.

"In countries like India and China, people can't or don't want to be reliant on their children now," said Mr. Hoskins of the International Social Security Association. But they remain in retirement limbo, waiting for governments and the private sector to act.

The New York Times, August 15, 1999
http://www.nytimes.com/library/review/081599retire-expectations-review.html

CRITICAL THINKING QUESTIONS

1. Discuss how the United States compares to other nations on the issue of retirement.
2. Explain the dilemma of ageism. How does this phenomenon affect the workplace?
3. How does a nation's life expectancy correlate with the national retirement age?
4. How has the perception of retirement changed over the years?

STORY-SPECIFIC QUESTIONS

1. Retirement has become a social value in many countries. Why then, is this social value being scrutinized for possible changes in the political and economic policy-making arenas?
2. What arguments are there for keeping people in the workforce longer than the traditional retirement age of 65?
3. Why would it be difficult to persuade Singaporeans to extend years in the workforce beyond age 60?

SHORT APPLICATION ASSIGNMENTS

1. In teams or individually, answer the story-specific questions; keep your answers to 25–75 words for each question.
2. In teams of three to five persons each, or as a whole class, discuss your responses to the critical thinking questions.
3. Prepare a one-page memo report (200–250 words) to your instructor in which you summarize this article. You will find a model one-page report on the Web site (nytimes.swcollege.com).
4. Write an executive summary (200–250 words). As an administrative assistant to a busy executive, you are expected to summarize selected articles and present important points. You will find a model executive summary on the Web site.
5. Summarize this article (100–125 words) for your company's newsletter. You will find a model newsletter on the Web site.
6. Write an essay (200–250 words) detailing how retirement has changed in the last few decades. What are reasons why people are retiring later in life? How do such delays affect the labor market for young, new employees?
7. Write a memo (500 words) defending or disputing the social security system. What are costs and benefits of this system, which provides payments to millions of Americans that are retired or unable to work?

BUILDING RESEARCH SKILLS

1. Individually or in teams, investigate the current problems facing the social security system. What are some "proposed" remedies? Who has proposed them and why? What kinds of opportunity costs will citizens encounter as a result of these suggested measures? Your instructor may ask you to submit a three- to five-page essay, post a Web page or report your results in a five-minute presentation, along with a letter of transmittal explaining your essay.
2. Individually or in teams, develop an alternative pension plan for individuals who retire before the national retirement age. How would this plan be unique or different for "younger" retiring employees versus those who have reached the traditional retirement age? What incentives would make this plan appealing? Your instructor may ask you to submit a three- to five-page essay, post a Web page or report your results in a five-minute presentation, along with a letter of transmittal explaining your essay.
3. Using at least three other references (e.g., books, research-journal articles, newspaper or magazine stories or credible Web sites), write an 800- to 1,000-word essay that addresses two of the critical thinking questions offered earlier. Assume that your essay will be used as an internal reference for a government's policy guidelines.
4. Using at least three other references (e.g., books, research-journal articles, newspaper or magazine stories or credible Web sites), post an 800- to 1,000-word Web page that addresses at least two of the earlier critical thinking questions. Assume that your page will be posted in the policy section of a government's intranet.

CHAPTER 5

Global Economics

PREVIEW

No nation has the requisite resources to economically produce within its borders all of the goods and services that its consumers want. In fact, essentially every nation depends on other countries for at least some raw materials or finished products. Few, if any, countries can ignore foreign trade in today's increasingly global economy. At the same time, however, economists continue to debate protectionism—governmental policies that limit or exclude imports.

On the one hand, some economists argue that expanding a national economy through foreign trade serves to strengthen industrial specialization and larger scale production. And they say foreign trade allows a country to specialize in those goods and services that it produces at a relatively low cost. Conversely, however, other economists argue that highly advanced countries are at a disadvantage because they cannot compete with the low wages that are paid to workers abroad, in the less developed countries.

A driving force, perhaps recklessly so, of the global economy is the unrestricted flow of capital among countries. Louis Uchitelle studies this freewheeling and rapid movement of money in his article "Crash Course: Just What's Driving the Crisis in Emerging Markets?"

China, due to its enormous size, is perhaps the largest of the world's emerging markets. In "U.S. Reaches an Accord to Open China Economy as Worldwide Market," Erik Eckholm and David E. Sanger report on the anticipated increase in trade relations to be created by this unprecedented agreement between China and America. David E. Sanger analyzes these same benefits in "A Deal the United States Just Couldn't Refuse."

Source: Christine M. Thompson/CyberTimes

Even without the trade agreement, China already has taken steps to increase its foreign trade. As Bob Tedeschi reports in "China Sets Up Its Own Web Site to Lure U.S. Concerns' Business," the Internet helps dissolve traditional physical borders among countries.

Crash Course: Just What's Driving the Crisis in Emerging Markets?

By Louis Uchitelle

Davos, Switzerland—Among the movers and shakers gathered here for the World Economic Forum, a striking metaphor is helping to frame the debate over the global financial crisis that began in Asia and has spread to several other developing countries. The debacle, some say, brings to mind a slick stretch of highway, scene of a half-dozen recent auto accidents. So is it careless driving or the highway that is the cause of the accidents?

Substitute freewheeling worldwide capital flows and unrestricted lending for the slippery, fast-moving highway. Make South Korea, Thailand, Indonesia, Russia and Brazil stand-ins for the drivers and their cars. The accidents are the panics and recessions—the crackups—that have devastated each of these countries. And the question now so widely debated is simple enough: Are the countries mostly to blame or the unrestricted capital flows, or both?

After the first accidents, the countries came in for almost all the blame. It was because of crony capitalism, bad banking and overleveraged real estate investments, many experts said. Fix the sloppy financial practices and also make enough bailout money available when a country gets into trouble—basically the current strategy of the International Monetary Fund for Brazil—and the accidents will be avoided or, at worst, will be mere fender benders.

But spectacular wrecks have occurred with alarming frequency and severity in the last 18 months, even in Brazil, and some who had mostly blamed the countries have begun to argue, here and in earlier interviews, that the system needs serious fixing, too.

The Clinton administration had placed most of the blame on the countries, and still does. But its view, like that of the IMF, is starting to reflect a more nuanced appraisal. "We have seen that countries need to pursue sounder policies and avoid lurching for short-term capital, as Mexico and Thailand did," said Lawrence Summers, the deputy treasury secretary. But in a phone interview this week from Washington, he also called for "more prudence on the part of the lenders."

And in the administration's most direct acknowledgment so far that it is not necessarily always committed to unrestricted capital flows, he added: "Where countries have controls that restrict short-term lending, we have not in general sought to dismantle them."

Some on Wall Street are similarly shifting ground. "It is appropriate to certainly consider fixing the system," said Stephen Roach, chief economist at Morgan Stanley Dean Witter. Morgan Stanley normally makes more money when capital flows freely and the firm can lend where and how it sees best.

But the recent string of crackups has given Roach second thoughts. "I am not completely convinced that restrictions on the system are necessary," he said, "but unstable capital flows have clearly been a precipitant of these crises."

At the top of many lists for fixing the system are proposals to limit the flow of short-term foreign loans to developing countries, loans that often contributed to more rapid growth but which piled up in huge amounts in Asia, Russia and Brazil. Then, at the first hint of trouble, much of the money fled, precipitating and worsening a full-scale financial collapse.

But other systemwide suggestions are winning favor as well: pursing flexible exchange rates, for example, to avoid sudden, frightening devaluations; introducing bankruptcy laws that let companies deep in foreign debt borrow and resume operations even before they pay off the old debts; and standstill provisions in lending agreements that would temporarily prevent a foreign lender from withdrawing loans from a South Korea or a Brazil in the midst of a crisis.

What they have in common is an effort to put more of the burden on international banks and other lenders to evaluate risks more carefully early on and suffer more of the consequences later if things go bad.

"The banks don't like this; they value liquidity of lending," said Barry Eichengreen, an international economist at the University of California at Berkeley. "But if they had a provision in their loan agreements that they cannot pull out their money right away when a crisis is developing, maybe they would not lend the money in the first place."

Some experts now favor rules that prevent not only foreign lenders but wealthy nationals—Brazilians, for example—from canceling their short-term loans and investments, then converting this money from local currencies into dollars and taking the dollars out of the country. Wealthy Brazilians, many of them already moving chunks of capital abroad, hold more than $150 billion in their government's debt and rushing this money out of the country would quickly exhaust Brazil's dollar reserves.

"My view is that basically all short-term debt constitutes potential capital flight," said Paul Krugman, an economist at the Massachusetts Institute of Technology. "Brazil is at risk not only from foreign lenders, but from anyone who can take money out of the country."

Perhaps some of these measures would make the highway safer for ordinary drivers. But before the dangerous stretch of road is rebuilt in hopes of preventing future accidents, the smashed cars of the last 18 months have to be repaired and put back in operation. There is little agreement on how to do that. Rather there are two diametrically opposite, so far unyielding, approaches.

The current practice, carried out at the insistence of the Clinton administration and the IMF, is to require countries in trouble to adopt policies intended to limit devaluations of a country's currency and restore the confidence of international lenders. If currencies plunge too far, the argument goes, then foreign loans become much harder to repay and inflation sets in as imports shoot up in price.

"The mainstream view would still be that the key solutions to crises remain policy adjustments within the countries themselves," said William Cline, chief economist at the Institute for International Finance, which represents lenders. "Once you restore confidence in a country's financial system, then you can get its economy growing again."

The chief tools in this approach are sharply higher interest rates and cutbacks in public spending. But the high rates and spending cutbacks invariably produce recessions.

The Clinton administration argues that once confidence in a financial system is restored, interest rates can then come down, as they have in South Korea and Thailand, and nations can begin the long climb out of recession. But even Thailand and South Korea are still on the side of the road, their economies spinning their wheels rather than moving forward again.

"It is too facile to say, 'Look at Korea and Thailand, they are turning around,'" said Dani Rodrik, a Harvard economist. "Their economies have taken bigger hits than either country has experienced in the last 30 years."

Like the East Asian countries, Brazil, the latest victim of a financial panic, is hewing to policies that are plunging that country into recession. And as the hobbling of giant Brazil slows economic activity everywhere in Latin America, the odds rise that even the United States and Europe could be caught in the spreading global crisis.

That would not happen so much because of recession in Latin America, but because some new blow—a major bankruptcy, for example, or a sharp decline in American stock prices—undermines confidence in an American financial system still nervous about Asia and Brazil.

The contrasting view is argued most vehemently by Jeffrey Sachs of Harvard, who insists that high interest rates and austerity measures are bringing disaster to many emerging markets. He would keep interest rates down to encourage economic activity and let exchange rates find their own level. A growing economy is more likely to restore investor confidence, he says, than a recessionary one burdened by high interest rates.

"The Treasury and the IMF have driven a large part of the developing world into recession," said Sachs, who directs Harvard's Institute for International Development. "And the Brazil case makes absolutely clear that the first step is not to defend overvalued currencies. The punishing cost of this is overwhelmingly high. This is a lesson that the IMF and the Treasury have continued to ignore. I don't understand why."

For all the disagreement over how to repair the damaged East Asian and Latin economies, much of the debate centers not on the present, but on how to avoid financial crises in the future. And here the proposals increasingly involve a mixture of fixing the system and fixing the countries—repairing the highway and making the drivers more cautious and skilled.

On the country side, several proposals have been made to set up a super central bank that would make huge amounts of money available to bail out a country in the event of a crisis. George Soros, the speculator and philanthropist, has offered one version, and another comes from Stanley Fischer, the IMF's first deputy managing director. But to qualify for such bailouts in the future, the countries would have to strengthen their banking and financial systems.

"You would shore up the international system by providing a more meaningful lender of last resort," said C. Fred Bergsten, director of the Institute for International Economics.

Those who focus mostly on the system would require, among other things, that banks put aside extra money in a reserve fund if they lent into emerging countries heavily burdened with foreign debt. "Putting aside money in that fashion reduces the profitability of a loan, which in turn makes lenders more cautious," said Ricardo French-Davis, a Chilean economist who works in Santiago with the U.N. Economic Commission for Latin America.

Krugman of MIT goes further in blaming the system and in arguing that the need to fix structural problems in individual countries should not stand in the way of broader macro-economic measures, particularly those designed to stimulate growth in hard times.

In the current issue of *Foreign Affairs*, he writes that over the last 25 years, much of the global economy has returned in many ways to a "pre-Depression free-market capitalism," with its virtues but also its vices—the main vice being a vulnerability to spectacular crackups.

"It is hard to avoid concluding that sooner or later we will have to turn the clock at least part of the way back," he writes. "To limit capital flows for countries that are unsuitable for either currency unions or free floating; to reregulate financial markets to some extent; and to seek low, but not too low, inflation rather than price stability. We must heed the lessons of Depression economics, lest we be forced to relearn them the hard way."

The New York Times, January 29, 1999
http://www.nytimes.com/library/world/global/012999econ-crises.html

CRITICAL THINKING QUESTIONS

1. Is borrowing from the IMF the best avenue a country should take when facing financial problems? Why, or why not?
2. What is your opinion of the strategies suggested for avoiding international financial collapse?
3. Why are economists cautious about establishing a "super bank" to bail nations out of dire financial straits?

STORY-SPECIFIC QUESTIONS

1. What were listed as causes of the multinational financial crisis?
2. What has been recommended to forego any future crises in the global market?
3. What expectations are established by the Clinton Administration to protect a country's financial stability?

SHORT APPLICATION ASSIGNMENTS

1. In teams or individually, answer the story-specific questions; keep your answers to 25–75 words for each question.
2. In teams of three to five persons each, or as a whole class, discuss your responses to the critical thinking questions.
3. Prepare a one-page memo report (200–250 words) to your instructor in which you summarize this article. You will find a model one-page report on the Web site (nytimes.swcollege.com).
4. Write an executive summary (200–250 words). As an administrative assistant to a busy executive, you are expected to summarize selected articles and present important points. You will find a model executive summary on the Web site.
5. Summarize this article (100–125 words) for your company's newsletter. You will find a model newsletter on the Web site.

BUILDING RESEARCH SKILLS

1. Individually or in teams, research the concept and the role of the International Monetary Fund (IMF). Based upon the information you gather, explain why this system is necessary for guarding against serious currency depreciation in the exchange markets. Your instructor may ask you to submit a three- to five-page essay, post a Web page or report your results in a five-minute presentation, along with a letter of transmittal explaining your essay.
2. Using at least three other references (e.g., books, research-journal articles, newspaper or magazine stories or credible Web sites), write an 800- to 1,000-word essay that addresses two of the critical thinking questions offered earlier. Assume that your essay will be used as an internal reference for a government's policy guidelines.
3. Using at least three other references (e.g., books, research-journal articles, newspaper or magazine stories or credible Web sites), post an 800- to 1,000-word Web page that addresses at least two of the earlier critical thinking questions. Assume that your page will be posted in the policy section of a government's intranet.

U.S. Reaches an Accord to Open China Economy as Worldwide Market

By Erik Eckholm with David E. Sanger

Beijing—American and Chinese negotiators reached a landmark agreement Monday that would open the economy of China, the world's most populous nation, to foreign competitors and would also make it a full partner in the world's trading system.

After six days of arduous negotiations, the United States trade representative, Charlene Barshefsky, and China's trade minister, Shi Guangsheng, signed the papers at 3:50 P.M., shook hands and raised a Champagne toast to an agreement that capped 13 years of on-and-off negotiations on China's entry into the World Trade Organization.

Under the deal, Beijing would reduce tariffs on various industrial and agricultural products. It would also lift many of the barriers that have hamstrung American banks and insurance and telephone companies that want to expand their operations and investments in China.

In exchange, the United States agreed to support China's bid for membership in the global trade group, the 135-member organization that sets the rules for international commerce.

China still must complete agreements with the European Union, Canada and some developing countries, including Brazil, before its application can be taken up by the group's member states.

"Let me just say that this is a profound and historic moment in U.S.-China relations," said a clearly exultant Barshefsky, adding that the agreement would not only aid the economies of both countries, but also serve as an anchor in their tumultuous political relationship.

The last six days of day-and-night negotiations were conducted in a "win-win spirit," Shi said, "and finally we reached an agreement that serves the interests of both China and the United States."

For all the rejoicing, the agreement faces tough resistance in the United States, where it is opposed by labor unions and some critics of China. Congress will not vote on the deal itself, but must vote to put an end to its annual review of Chinese trade and to establish normal—and permanent—trade relations with Beijing.

For China, membership in the trade group would mean a long-sought acceptance into the "club" of world powers. The WTO's elaborate rules would help protect China from unfair trade policies abroad, but would also impose a body of international rules on China's own fitful progress toward a market economy.

The accord goes to the heart of China's transition to an open, market economy. It would put Beijing, for the first time, under the jurisdiction of the rules set by the World Trade Organization, which are enforced by a trade court.

Full membership would be a victory for President Jiang Zemin, who sees achieving economic modernization as his legacy even as he tries to ensure continuation of Communist rule. At the same time, membership would cheer the more liberal, reform-oriented factions led by Prime Minister Zhu Rongji, since it locks China onto a path that could force China's state-owned industries to become efficient.

The step is a politically risky one for China, coming at a time when those state-run companies are already shedding millions of workers.

For President Clinton, Monday's agreement provides a badly needed centerpiece to his fraying policy of engagement with China, offering the prospect of tangible gains to many companies and to consumers. It is also a stunning recovery from what his own top aides describe as a huge mistake: his decision to walk away from the surprisingly sweeping deal, largely identical to Monday's, offered in April by Zhu.

After the signing Monday, Barshefsky and Gene Sperling, the White House chief of economic policy—who opposed the April deal and attended the talks as a symbol of Clinton's renewed commitment—were driven to the secluded leadership compound for a brief meeting with Jiang, who twice in the past month conducted telephone talks with Clinton.

Speaking in Turkey Monday, Clinton said: "I think this is a good agreement for China, for America and for the world."

But Clinton's struggle to make this accord a central foreign policy achievement is far from over.

Congress will essentially review the accord when it prepares to vote on the biggest single American concession: granting permanent trading rights to China rather than reviewing those rights annually, a Capitol Hill ritual that has turned into an annual debate about human rights and arms proliferation.

Clinton has spoken often of "integrating China into the world economy" and gradually getting the country to embrace "the rule of law," starting with commercial law. But without closing a World Trade Organization agreement, his aides said, he would have little progress to point to.

The agreement may also help to repair the damage done to Chinese-American relations by charges of Chinese spying in the United States, the American bombing of the Chinese Embassy in Belgrade in May and China's continuing suspicion that the United States is attempting to "contain" Chinese military and economic power.

"Successful completion of WTO will go a long way to smooth out some of the extreme oscillation that we have seen in Sino-American relations in recent years," said Joseph Fewsmith, a China expert at Boston University. "I think it gives us a chance to build some substance into a relationship that has been badly damaged."

Monday's agreement is a huge step toward membership for China, but it very likely comes too late, experts said, for China to be admitted before November 30, when a new round of global trade talks begins in Seattle.

But Monday's accord means that China can take a larger role in setting the agenda there. And past trade rounds have lasted for years.

From the beginning, the American goal was not just to press China for large reductions in tariffs on imported farm products and industrial goods like automobiles. In measures that may ultimately have a far more profound impact, China had to commit itself to allowing foreign companies to take majority investments in many industrial and service sectors.

The final six days, and usually nights, of negotiations went through several rough spots. Several times Barshefsky and Sperling suggested they were packing up to leave, threats Barshefsky said in an interview Monday were "largely tactical, to force the Chinese to make some progress."

"Clearly," she said, "they were not going to let us leave."

In an interview from Hong Kong Monday, Barshefsky said that the key Chinese player in the talks appeared to be Prime Minister Zhu, who twice stepped in to break an impasse and ultimately directed his negotiators to make several key concessions—allowing American companies to take a 50 percent stake in China's booming telecommunications companies, for example. But all his decisions, analysts here said, were almost certainly cleared by the top party leadership.

The outlines of an agreement had been worked out last April, when Zhu visited Washington. But President Clinton backed away from any agreement at the time, fearing Congressional opposition. Most of Monday's pact follows the April understandings, and in resolving areas of continued dispute, Barshefsky asserted—in a statement sure to be scrutinized by skeptics in Congress—"I think we achieved an overall strengthening of this agreement."

The agreement involves a general reduction in China's import tariffs from the current average of 22.1 percent down to 17 percent, with tariffs on major American farm products cut sharply to 15 percent or less.

Tariffs on automobile imports, which now range up to 100 percent to protect China's inefficient producers, would be reduced over a six-year period to 25 percent, with the quickest reduction in the initial years. That is one year longer than China offered in April.

But equally important, American officials said, foreign auto companies and banks would for the first time be able to offer consumer loans for cars, a critical concession in a country where few can lay out the money for such a large purchase.

Thus, Chinese consumers may soon be buying General Motors cars, for example, with the "G.M.A.C." loans so familiar to Americans.

Two of the most contentious issues in recent days, Barshefsky said, involved the American demands for ways to respond to surges of imports into the

United States and for use of a method to identify when the Chinese might be illegally selling products below cost, or "dumping."

China wanted such measures to phase out quickly, but in the end agreed to surge protections for a 12-year period, and the anti-dumping regime for 15 years. Without those concessions, Barshefsky told her Chinese counterparts, Congress could easily balk at the accord.

For the first time, China also agreed to allow foreign companies to distribute their own goods, rather than forcing them to distribute food or industrial components through Chinese companies. They would also be able to repair and support their products directly.

In terms of textiles, one of the most politically sensitive topics in the United States, it was the Americans calling for restrictions on free trade. The Chinese wanted to scale back the American demand to continue existing textile import quotas for another 10 years. In the end, the United States agreed to end quotas after five years, but with special anti-surge safeguards for another four years after that.

The anti-dumping and textile provisions are charged issues for Vice President Al Gore. He hopes to keep the support of organized labor in his presidential bid, but such groups oppose the trade accord.

Foreign investment in China's telecommunications sector had become a sore point inside China, where some saw it as an issue of national security. The Americans fought for 51 percent ownership rights—which Zhu had offered in April—but finally agreed that foreign firms could take up to 50 percent ownership of companies in this booming sector, beginning two years after China enters the trade organization.

"It became clear that this was an incredibly emotional issue for the Chinese," Sperling said in an interview.

Important provisions would open Chinese retail banking to foreign firms over several years, and also improve market access for insurance companies, and legal and accounting firms. But the American negotiators got far less in China's infant and high-risk financial securities market, where they would be limited to minority stakes in activities like underwriting stock issues.

For China—which is still unraveling the legacy of Mao Zedong's cloistered, command economy—entry into the World Trade Organization will carry profound implications.

Many economists here compare entry to Deng Xiaoping's landmark opening of the economy to market forces and foreign influence in the late 1970s.

"The opening of China to the outside world began with Mao Zedong's meeting with Richard Nixon in 1972," said Hu Angang, a leading economist here at the Chinese Academy of Sciences.

"The second major stage was marked by Deng Xiaoping's visit to the United States in 1979."

"Joining WTO will represent a whole new stage in China's opening to the world," he said. "It will signify a shift from partial to comprehensive opening and reform," he said, "and a shift from an opening based on domestic rules to an opening based on internationally defined rules."

China's embrace of more open markets reflects the desire of President Jiang and other top leaders to push ahead with a radical overhaul of the domestic economy, opening it to global competition and bringing in more foreign capital and technology.

President Jiang and his fellow Communist Party leaders see economic transformation as vital if China is to become a great power in the century ahead. They also know that if they do not provide steadily rising incomes to their people, the party's rule is in trouble.

So the renewed opening is perhaps unavoidable, but it is a risky step for the leaders, who can expect to see some cherished state enterprises crushed even as others are energized.

In the short run, at least, already impoverished farmers may be harmed by cheap imports and more urban workers might lose their jobs.

The impact of Monday's agreement on the power of Zhu, who is nominally number three in the party hierarchy, is unclear. Over the last six months or so, his influence appeared to slip, as the country took a more conservative and nationalistic turn, and Jiang took a stronger role in economic matters. By many accounts, Zhu lost his former control over policy on the World Trade Organization and the reform of state enterprises.

But Ms. Barshefsky said Monday that in a phone call between Clinton and Jiang last month, "Jiang said that Zhu Rongji is in charge of these negotiations."

"And," she said, "it looked very much as if he had taken ownership of it."

Monday's agreement put Zhu and his ideas back in the limelight, but Chinese television reports this evening featured President Jiang, and both Chinese and foreign analysts continue to speculate about power shifts in the secretive Communist hierarchy.

On paper, the changes China has promised are breathtaking in scope. But even the most optimistic American officials concede that threatened ministries and provinces are likely to find ways to delay implementation of many provisions. This suspicion is likely to feed controversy in the United States about the pact.

Still, both Democrats and Republicans say the agreement will almost certainly be approved in Congress sometime early next year, after a spirited debate.

The New York Times, November 16, 1999
http://www.nytimes.com/library/world/asia/111699china-us-trade.html

CRITICAL THINKING QUESTIONS

1. What, in your opinion, will be the apparent difficulties with implementing the trade agreement with China? What steps must be taken for ease of implementation?

2. What role, if any, should the World Trade Organization (WTO) play in negotiating this agreement?
3. What are the strongest "political" arguments for the U.S.-China agreement? What are the strongest "political" arguments against it?
4. Who will be the winners and losers in this agreement? Why?

STORY-SPECIFIC QUESTIONS

1. Summarize the provisions of the trade agreement crafted by representatives from China and the United States.
2. Will this agreement mean that the WTO will be able to intervene in domestic issues in China? Explain.
3. Why is the agreement important for China's economic and political future?

SHORT APPLICATION ASSIGNMENTS

1. In teams or individually, answer the story-specific questions; keep your answers to 25–75 words for each question.
2. In teams of three to five persons each, or as a whole class, discuss your responses to the critical thinking questions.
3. Prepare a one-page memo report (200–250 words) to your instructor in which you summarize this article. You will find a model one-page report on the Web site (nytimes.swcollege.com).
4. Write an executive summary (200–250 words). As an administrative assistant to a busy executive, you are expected to summarize selected articles and present important points. You will find a model executive summary on the Web site.
5. Summarize this article (100–125 words) for your company's newsletter. You will find a model newsletter on the Web site.

BUILDING RESEARCH SKILLS

1. Individually or in teams, investigate the current trade deficit with China. What has the United States done and what should it do to reduce this deficit? Your instructor may ask you to submit a three- to five-page essay, post a Web page or report your results in a five-minute presentation, along with a letter of transmittal explaining your essay.
2. Using at least three other references (e.g., books, research-journal articles, newspaper or magazine stories or credible Web sites), write an 800- to 1,000-word essay that addresses two of the critical thinking questions offered earlier. Assume that your essay will be used as an internal reference for a government's policy guidelines.
3. Using at least three other references (e.g., books, research-journal articles, newspaper or magazine stories or credible Web sites), post an 800- to 1,000-word Web page that addresses at least two of the earlier critical thinking questions. Assume that your page will be posted in the policy section of a government's intranet.

A Deal the United States Just Couldn't Refuse

By David E. Sanger

Washington—In the end, the deal struck Monday between the United States and China was one that President Clinton had little choice but to seal.

For a president who talks constantly these days about harnessing the forces of economic globalization, the agreement to integrate China into the global trading system marked the culmination of Clinton's single biggest imprint on American foreign policy: the use of American economic power for strategic ends. That is what this agreement is all about, locking in China's commitment to economic reforms and with it, he is betting, a further opening of Chinese society.

But Clinton came to that strategy in the most roundabout of ways. He began from the other side of the China debate, denouncing President Bush for economic engagement with a nation that had just killed hundreds at Tiananmen Square. Soon he came to the conclusion that every president has reached since Richard Nixon: There is little realistic choice other than engagement.

A year and a half into his presidency, Clinton had already reversed course, saying he would no longer link human rights or missile proliferation or other issues to his annual renewal of China's trading rights with the United States. Ever since, he has been a passionate advocate of the long-term benefits of opening up China's politics by opening up its markets—stringing American-built cell-phone networks from Shanghai to Tibet, letting a hundred Internet sites bloom, insisting that if China applies the rule of law for Boeing, it eventually will have to apply it to dissidents.

He has, in short, pressed the economic engagement argument to an extreme no other president, Bush included, has ever taken. Along the way he has learned a hard lesson: His early hopes that economic change and political change would quickly come hand-in-hand in China were a fantasy. In the end, he concluded that if the business of America is business, so was much of its foreign policy.

Last week, for example, China's leaders thought nothing of simultaneously negotiating with Charlene Barshefsky, the U.S. trade representative, over subjecting China to the WTO's commercial laws while sentencing four members of the Falun Gong, the religious group whose silent meditations have struck fear into the heart of the Communist Party, to prison sentences of up to 12 years. The first was good business, a way of promoting more foreign investment into a country that needs the world's cash and technology more than ever. The second was, in the view of China's leaders, a question of political control. Clinton has now molded American policy to reflect that reality.

"We have to be realistic about the prospects for change in China because there are elements of the country that will never change," Ms. Barshefsky said Monday. "But what's the alternative? Let's punish China by not gaining access to its market? Who does that punish? I am cautious in making claims that a market-opening agreement leads to anything other than opening the market. It may—it could have a spillover effect—but it may not. And we've got to understand that."

Perhaps it reflects a maturing of the China debate in the United States that just as Clinton has come to understand the limits of trade agreements, some of his critics have come to appreciate their possibilities. Human Rights Watch, one of the many organizations constantly monitoring the country, embraced the accord Monday, sounding a note of cautious hope that Clinton's long-term bet could pay off.

"China's membership in the WTO could increase pressure for greater openness, more press freedom, enhanced rights for workers and an independent judiciary," Human Rights Watch said in a statement.

There are elements of Monday's agreement that could do just that—if one is willing to wait long enough.

For example, Barshefsky's negotiating team spent a considerable amount of time defanging China's insistence over the summer that foreigners could never invest in Chinese Internet service providers. The United States insisted that the Internet had to be dealt with like the rest of the telecommunications market— open to foreigners and Chinese alike. That is a remarkable concession in a country that only a few years ago strictly controlled who could own radios and that put speakers in every village, to blare propaganda.

"In an increasingly information-based economy it is difficult to tell people to be economically creative and politically suppressed," the national security adviser, Sandy Berger, said Monday from Turkey, where he is traveling with Clinton. "But it's a long-term hypothesis."

Just as importantly, the Chinese gave away their ability to be the sole judge of what foreign investors can do and what they cannot. Once China is a member of the WTO, it must submit to the group's dispute-settlement system. That means cases of Chinese trade barriers will be sent to three-judge panels in Geneva.

No one expects that the Chinese leadership will roll over and do whatever the courts command. But then again, neither do the Europeans.

In short, there is hope but no assurance that trade liberalization can lock in political liberalization. But there is a far better bet that it may be able to lock in China's economic liberalizations.

Over the next five years the accord will throw open to foreigners—at least on paper—markets that have long been out of reach. Life insurance companies will have the right to sell their policies anywhere in the country. Grain producers and computer makers can distribute their goods themselves, without going through state-owned firms. Five years from now foreign banks will be able to open branches, doing business with ordinary Chinese in the national currency, the yuan.

Each of these businesses have long been protected by the Chinese government. By throwing open the doors, after five years of preparations, China's leaders are clearly betting that the arrival of the foreigners will spur both efficiency and growth. It demonstrates, experts say, that China has learned a lesson from the experiences of Japan and South Korea: Over-protection of domestic industries breeds fat, smug companies that are ripe for disaster when hard times strike.

It is a risky strategy for the Chinese, of course. Competition can breed unemployment—already a growing problem in China—and unemployment can breed political activism.

But it is also a risk for the United States.

"We're seeing a backlash against too much trade liberalization too fast," said Jeffrey Garten, the former undersecretary of commerce and one of the architects of Clinton's early forays into commercial diplomacy.

It is a backlash already in full swing in Europe, and parts of Asia. If it hits particularly hard in China, Washington may be reassessing the political benefits of Clinton's strategy.

The New York Times, November 16, 1999
http://www.nytimes.com/library/world/asia/111699china-us-assess.html

CRITICAL THINKING QUESTIONS

1.   What do you foresee as the most important outcome of this agreement?
2.   Should the WTO have input into China's domestic affairs (e.g., human rights) because of this agreement? Why, or why not?
3.   What are the economic and political risks for the United States with this deal? What are the economic and political risks for China?

STORY-SPECIFIC QUESTIONS

1.   What does the Clinton Administration believe will be significant gains from the trade agreement?
2.   For what reasons did the United States change its position on economic engagement in China under President Clinton's leadership?
3.   What are examples of markets that will be available to Chinese citizens after this agreement is finalized?

SHORT APPLICATION ASSIGNMENTS

1.   In teams or individually, answer the story-specific questions; keep your answers to 25–75 words for each question.

2. In teams of three to five persons each, or as a whole class, discuss your responses to the critical thinking questions.

3. Prepare a one-page memo report (200–250 words) to your instructor in which you summarize this article. You will find a model one-page report on the Web site (nytimes.swcollege.com).

4. Write an executive summary (200–250 words). As an administrative assistant to a busy executive, you are expected to summarize selected articles and present important points. You will find a model executive summary on the Web site.

5. Summarize this article (100–125 words) for your company's newsletter. You will find a model newsletter on the Web site.

BUILDING RESEARCH SKILLS

1. In teams, investigate the costs and benefits of international trade. Prepare a panel discussion with at least three other students in which you present your views on the costs and benefits of trade.

2. Individually or in teams, investigate the current trade deficit with China. What has the United States done and what should it do to reduce this deficit? Your instructor may ask you to submit a three- to five-page essay, post a Web page or report your results in a five-minute presentation, along with a letter of transmittal explaining your essay.

3. Using at least three other references (e.g., books, research-journal articles, newspaper or magazine stories or credible Web sites), write an 800- to 1,000-word essay that addresses two of the critical thinking questions offered earlier. Assume that your essay will be used as an internal reference for a government's policy guidelines.

4. Using at least three other references (e.g., books, research-journal articles, newspaper or magazine stories or credible Web sites), post an 800- to 1,000-word Web page that addresses at least two of the earlier critical thinking questions. Assume that your page will be posted in the policy section of a government's intranet.

China Sets Up Its Own Web Site to Lure U.S. Concerns' Business

By Bob Tedeschi

In the first official foray into electronic commerce for the world's fastest-growing economy, the Government of China has set up an Internet site intended to help its companies market goods to American corporations.

The site, www.meetchina.com, which was announced Sunday, is operated for China by U.S. Business Network Inc., a San Francisco-based company.

According to Ken Leonard, the company's chief executive, the site will be a clearinghouse of sorts for businesses in mainland China that wish to connect with American customers via the Internet.

The Chinese government will help U.S. Business Network solicit companies that will pay $1,500 to $3,000 to participate in the site, and receive help developing American contacts, with 20 percent of the proceeds going to the government. Participating Chinese companies will be able to post information about themselves and their products or services, along with contact information that includes e-mail addresses.

Until recently, Leonard said, Chinese companies were not allowed to make direct contact with foreign companies, but instead were required to first seek export licenses from the government. In recent months, the China has been more liberal in issuing such licenses, particularly for smaller companies, and dealing directly with Western businesses. It is smaller companies that China is trying to promote through the new site, he said.

"From China's perspective, it fits perfectly," said Patrick Meehan, research director for the Gartner Group, a technology consulting firm. "It's kind of open, but not all the way. It's part of the 'great firewall of China' strategy, where they have a way to funnel information in and out of the country."

According to Michael Borrus, co-director of the Berkeley Roundtable on the International Economy, the site's launch is more notable for its political implications than as a breakthrough on e-commerce. Observing that the government has been trying to privatize China's state-owned industries, Borrus said, "This will facilitate that process by pushing them to reform via contact with the West."

"It also falls into the classic Chinese model of dabbling in something long enough to see the various impacts before you commit to it completely," Borrus said.

Leonard, who lobbied the Chinese government for a year before receiving its go-ahead, said the site would focus first on Chinese businesses that are involved in the information technology industry. He added that the site was being marketed on the Internet—through banner advertisements on Yahoo, for example.

The New York Times, April 12, 1999
http://www.nytimes.com/library/tech/99/04/biztech/articles/12site.html

CRITICAL THINKING QUESTIONS

1. Why do you believe this Web site will help or hurt small business privatization in China?
2. What will be the advantages of Chinese businesses facilitating business on-line with U.S. companies?
3. What other Chinese domestic issues will likely be instrumental in getting this Web site up and running? Why?

STORY-SPECIFIC QUESTIONS

1. What does the Chinese government hope to gain by establishing a Web site?
2. What types of companies are initially being included as part of the Chinese Web site?
3. What will participating Chinese companies be able to do on this Web site?

SHORT APPLICATION ASSIGNMENTS

1. In teams or individually, answer the story-specific questions; keep your answers to 25–75 words for each question.
2. In teams of three to five persons each, or as a whole class, discuss your responses to the critical thinking questions.
3. Prepare a one-page memo report (200–250 words) to your instructor in which you summarize this article. You will find a model one-page report on the Web site (nytimes.swcollege.com).
4. Write an executive summary (200–250 words). As an administrative assistant to a busy executive, you are expected to summarize selected articles and present important points. You will find a model executive summary on the Web site.
5. Summarize this article (100–125 words) for your company's newsletter. You will find a model newsletter on the Web site.

BUILDING RESEARCH SKILLS

1. Individually or in teams, search the *New York Times on the Web* (http://search.nytimes.com/search/daily/) for at least three articles on U.S. trade relations with China. Your instructor may ask you to submit a three- to five-page summary of these articles, post a Web page or report your results in a five-minute presentation, along with a letter of transmittal explaining your summary.

2. Individually or in teams, explore the Meet China Web site (http://www.meetchina. com). What are the different sections? How is the site organized? Is it easy to navigate? As a U.S. business looking to do business in China, would you find this site valuable? Why, or why not? Your instructor may ask you to submit a three- to five-page analysis or report your results in a five-minute presentation, along with a letter of transmittal explaining your results.

3. Using at least three other references (e.g., books, research-journal articles, newspaper or magazine stories or credible Web sites), write an 800- to 1,000-word essay that addresses two of the critical thinking questions offered earlier. Assume that your essay will be used as an internal reference for a government's policy guidelines.

4. Using at least three other references (e.g., books, research-journal articles, newspaper or magazine stories or credible Web sites), post an 800- to 1,000-word Web page that addresses at least two of the earlier critical thinking questions. Assume that your page will be posted in the policy section of a government's intranet.

CHAPTER 6

Other Economics Issues

PREVIEW

Throughout history, from small-scale businesses to major industries, technology has increased productivity. Turning human work over to machines—the process of "mechanization"—has served to improve the efficiency of producing and distributing products. And thanks to computers and Internet technology, new production and distribution models are flourishing. This increased productivity, however, is getting mixed reviews.

Many critics have called for more control and oversight to ensure that people are treated equitably in this rapidly growing, cyber-based market of producers and consumers. While they see more governmental intervention as the key, those on the other side of the issue argue that too much intervention (e.g., taxation and monitoring) intrudes on and stifles free enterprise. The field of economics helps decision-makers measure and develop policies for this latest round of technological productivity.

The economists interviewed for "Productivity as the Catalyst of Prosperity" note that computerization seems to be spurring productivity. Likewise, Steve Lohr, in his article "Computer Age Gains Respect of Economists," also reports that even skeptical economists are grudgingly acknowledging the importance of computers and related technologies. They say that at the very least, computers could bring marginal benefits to productivity.

Source: Christine M. Thompson/CyberTimes

But who eventually pays for these benefits? Jeri Clausing's articles "Debate on Internet Taxes Take Political Turn" and "Internet Tax Panel Faces Thorny Issues" discuss the dilemma Congress faces—deciding if and how to tax Internet communications and commerce.

Productivity as the Catalyst of Prosperity

By Deborah Stead

Like scientists poring over a petri dish and quarreling about what the microscope shows, economists these days have been squinting at the "new era" economy to spot a sign—any sign—of the kind of growth that really matters. Yes, output is swelling and jobs are multiplying, the stock market is robust and inflation dormant. But what about productivity?

After all, a steady rise in output per employee is an essential enzyme for a strong economy. Without it, gross domestic product gains and job growth won't bring the higher standard of living associated with national prosperity.

And is productivity finally growing beyond the paltry annual average of 1 percent or so of the last two decades? That's what the optimists and the pessimists are slugging out.

In *Prosperity: The Coming 20-Year Boom and What It Means to You* (Times Books, $27.50), Bob Davis and David Wessel ultimately side with the optimists, even though they don't see many productivity gains yet.

Instead, in this engrossing, well-reported book, the authors—both economics correspondents at *The Wall Street Journal*—argue that during the next 20 years, computerization will finally deliver its long-awaited productivity payoff.

They also predict the blooming of a widely shared prosperity, a result of this productivity spurt, broader post-secondary education and—get this—globalization.

"The next 10 to 20 years will see the flowering of an era," they write, "in contrast to the economic disappointments of the past 25."

All this, of course, fights the gloomier view that technology and globalization will only widen the gap between the rich and the rest of the country. But Mr. Davis and Mr. Wessel, whose book grew out of issues they covered in 1995, set out to prove that history is on their side.

Drawing on company archives and on the work of economists like Paul David at Stanford University, the authors maintain that computers are where electricity was at the turn of the century: a nifty new technology but not yet used well enough to affect productivity.

Not until the 1920's, they say, did electricity produce sizable productivity gains.

To argue their point, the authors take a fascinating trip to turn-of-the-century Newton, Iowa, where the Maytag company was making farm machines.

Shaft-and-belt systems (yesterday's mainframes) were just yielding clumsily to individual motors (read, desktops) in the factory, and Thomas Edison aggressively marketed new systems that weren't really ready.

The big debate was over alternating versus direct current, the Mac-versus-PC fight of that era.

Slowly, though, electricity spread to become a fact instead of a feature of production. By the 1920s, Maytag was churning out affordable washing machines in Newton, while Ford cars were zipping off the assembly line in Detroit. It takes decades for technology to produce prosperity, the authors say, as they trace similar stop-and-start progress in computerization.

And why will the wealth from computerization be so widely spread? Because of more widely available post-secondary education, the authors say, notably at the nation's 1,100 community colleges. These schools are largely unappreciated by state legislators, the authors lament, even though "what goes on at a school like Cuyahoga Community College, in Cleveland and similar institutions across the country is more important to the American middle class than what happens at Harvard."

Such colleges, now with five million students, prepare new and displaced workers for the technology-heavy economy to come. And as such employees flood the job market, the premium price paid for "educated" workers will start to disappear and the now-widening income gap will narrow.

That is what happened in the 1920s, the authors show, when high schools, once thought a luxury, were regularly graduating working-class students instead of just the college-bound children of the elite.

Computers will ultimately require less expertise anyway, the authors say, thanks to ease-of-use inventions incubated in the Army and the world of the disabled.

As for the effects of globalization, Mr. Davis and Mr. Wessel use reporting and reasoning that are a bit less reassuring, though still respectable. They try to show why foreign investment is a boon in places like Tennessee, why imports are prosperity's allies and why free trade is not anti-worker, as it is often painted. Computer programmers in Bangalore, India, won't take cutting-edge software contracts away from Americans; such offshore programming is grunt work, not innovation. (To be fair, the authors acknowledge that pundits once talked this way about Japanese manufacturers.)

"We could be wrong, of course," they say about their prosperity theory. A major war could wreck global trade, they note, or the Federal Reserve might unwisely put the brakes on the economy, or China and India could turn into Japanese-style competition for America.

But if some of the book's premises seem more solid than others, no matter. "Prosperity" pulls together many threads to become a primer of sorts, a framework for figuring out how an economy could work for everyone.

The New York Times, April 5, 1998
http://www.nytimes.com/library/financial/sunday/040598spend-shel.html

CRITICAL THINKING QUESTIONS

1. Explain how economic growth shapes the "American" quality of life. Has this growth been beneficial to all Americans? Explain.
2. Can we attribute most of America's prosperity to technology? Why, or why not?
3. What does globalization mean? What are the various aspects of globalization?

STORY-SPECIFIC QUESTIONS

1. What are predictions for economic growth/productivity in the next 20 years?
2. How will technology and globalization impact the overall quality of life for each income bracket?
3. Explain how the introduction of electricity is analogous to the rise of technology.

SHORT APPLICATION ASSIGNMENTS

1. In teams or individually, answer the story-specific questions; keep your answers to 25–75 words for each question.
2. In teams of three to five persons each, or as a whole class, discuss your responses to the critical thinking questions.
3. Prepare a one-page memo report (200–250 words) to your instructor in which you summarize this article. You will find a model one-page report on the Web site (nytimes.swcollege.com).
4. Write an executive summary (200–250 words). As an administrative assistant to a busy executive, you are expected to summarize selected articles and present important points. You will find a model executive summary on the Web site.
5. Summarize this article (100–125 words) for your company's newsletter. You will find a model newsletter on the Web site.

BUILDING RESEARCH SKILLS

1. Individually or in teams, search The Bureau of Labor Statistics (http://stats.bls.gov/) for at least three reports on productivity. Your instructor may ask you to submit a three- to five-page summary of these articles, post a Web page or report your results in a five-minute presentation, along with a letter of transmittal explaining your summary.
2. Using at least three other references (e.g., books, research-journal articles, newspaper or magazine stories or credible Web sites), write an 800- to 1,000-word essay that addresses two of the critical thinking questions offered earlier. Assume that your essay will be used as an internal reference for a government's policy guidelines.
3. Using at least three other references (e.g., books, research-journal articles, newspaper or magazine stories or credible Web sites), post an 800- to 1,000-word Web page that addresses at least two of the earlier critical thinking questions. Assume that your page will be posted in the policy section of a government's intranet.

Computer Age Gains Respect of Economists

By Steve Lohr

In a nation of technophiles, where Internet millionaires are minted daily, it seems heresy to question the economic payoff from information technology—the billions upon billions spent each year by companies and households on everything from computers to software to cell phones.

But for more than a decade, most of the nation's leading economists have been heretics. They have not been much impressed by the high-tech dogma—embraced by corporate executives, business school professors and Wall Street alike—that regards the transformation of the economy through the magic of information technology as a self-evident truth.

"You can see the Computer Age everywhere," Robert Solow, a Nobel prize-winner from the Massachusetts Institute of Technology wrote a few years ago, "but in the productivity statistics."

For years, even as the computer revolutionized the workplace, productivity—the output of goods and services per worker—stagnated, barely advancing 1 percent a year. So it is easy to see how Solow's pithy comment became the favorite punchline of the economic naysayers.

Yet today, even renowned skeptics on the subject of technology's contribution to the economy, like Solow, are having second thoughts. Productivity growth has picked up, starting in 1996, capped by a surge in the second half of last year, after eight years of economic expansion. That has drawn attention because past upward swings in productivity typically occurred early in a recovery as economic activity rebounded. Once companies increased hiring, it slowed again.

But something seems fundamentally different this time, something apparently having a lot to do with the increased speed and efficiency that the Internet and other pervasive information-technology advances are bringing to the mundane day-to-day tasks of millions of businesses.

The question, posed by economists, is whether the higher productivity growth, averaging about 2 percent in the last three years, roughly double the pace from 1973 to 1995, is the long-awaited confirmation that the nation's steadily rising investment in computers and communications is finally paying off. The evidence is starting to point in that direction.

"My beliefs are shifting on this subject," said Solow. "I am still far from certain. But the story always was that it took a long time for people to use information technology and truly become more efficient. That story sounds a lot more convincing today than it did a year or two ago."

Another pillar in the pessimist camp was Daniel Sichel, an economist at the Federal Reserve. His work, along with another Fed economist, Stephen Oliner, in 1994, and on his own in 1997, found that computers contributed little to productivity growth. But recently, Sichel ran similar calculations for the last few years and came to a different conclusion.

In a paper that has just been published in the quarterly *Business Economics*, Sichel wrote that his new work points to "a striking step up in the contribution of computers to output growth." And the nation's improved productivity performance, he noted, is "raising the possibility that businesses are finally reaping the benefits of information technology."

The impact of information technology on the economy is more than an academic debate. If, as some experts assert, the technology dividend is a key reason for the nation's extraordinary run of high growth, rising wages and low inflation, there are significant policy implications. If the recent gains are not just a temporary blip, it suggests that the Federal Reserve can be less fearful of inflation and keep interest rates stable rather than be forced to raise them to cool off what would otherwise be considered an overheated economy.

Indeed, the Fed chairman, Alan Greenspan, and the other Fed governors are scheduled to hear presentations on information technology's effect on the economy from several academics during a private meeting in Washington on Thursday.

Greenspan, for one, seems to believe a fundamental change is under way. He told Congress early this year that the economy was enjoying "higher, technology-driven productivity growth."

The Fed governors will hear a forceful case for technological optimism from Erik Brynjolfsson, an associate professor at the MIT Sloan School of Management.

Brynjolfsson asserts that the economic value of speed, quality improvements, customer service and new products are often not captured by government statistics. "These are the competitive advantages of information technology," he said. "We need a broader definition of output in this new economy, which goes beyond the industrial-era concept of widgets coming off the assembly line."

The government, after years of defending its figures, conceded two weeks ago that productivity growth may be understated. The core of the problem, government economists say, is the increasingly complex challenge of defining and measuring output in much of the economy's fast-growing service sector, which includes the vast reaches of banking, finance, health care and education.

According to the official statistics, a bank today is only about 80 percent as productive as a bank in 1977. Yet that seems to take scant account of, say, 24-hour automated teller machines, which clearly benefit customers who no longer have to wait in lines to be served by human tellers during regular "bankers' hours."

Edwin Dean, chief of the productivity division of the Bureau of Labor Statistics, wrote in a new research paper that the agency was increasingly concerned that its measurements did not "fully reflect changes in the quality of goods and services" or "capture the full impact of new technology on economic performance."

Still, the government's methods of measurement will not be overhauled anytime soon. "These are tough, tough questions and we are not going to get instant solutions," Dean explained in an interview.

American corporations long ago made up their minds, voting for technology with their dollars. Investment in information technology—computing and telecommunications gear—has quadrupled over the last decade, rising as a share of all business spending on equipment from 29 percent to 53 percent, according to the Commerce Department. And that is only the hardware. There have been similar surges in corporate spending on software, consulting, technical support and training related to the field.

"The payoff from information technology is unquestionably there with individual companies and we're seeing it over and over again," said Chuck Rieger, a senior consultant at IBM's services division.

Of course, anecdotal evidence from individual companies is no proof of broad-based benefits in an $8.5-trillion economy. But what many experts find encouraging is that the rapid introduction of low-cost Internet technology means most companies can now afford to set up electronic links with customers and suppliers. For example, a recent survey of 2,500 manufacturing companies, conducted by PricewaterhouseCoopers, found that the number of factories with Internet links to customers and suppliers doubled last year.

At more and more companies, these Internet-based networks are already streamlining the mundane chores of business life like invoicing, purchasing and inventory control. This is not the glamorous side of Internet commerce, occupied by Amazon.com and others selling consumer products. Yet if a technology dividend in productivity is at hand, the place to look is in the back offices of business. "That is where it will be," Solow, the MIT economists, said, "in the wholesale automation of corporate transactions."

This business-to-business commerce over the Internet is projected to jump from $48 billion in 1998 to $1.5 trillion by 2003, according to Forrester Research Inc. During the same period, the research firm estimates that consumer sales over Internet will rise from $3.9 billion to $108 billion.

The service sector of the economy is where productivity gains appear to have been especially sluggish and where experts are looking most closely for evidence of an efficiency payoff from technology.

In Chicago, Michael Rushmore, a banker, speaks of how Internet computing has "fundamentally changed the way we do business" over the last three or four years. Take the way corporate loans are syndicated among many banks, notes Rushmore, a managing director of Nationsbanc Montgomery Securities, the securities arm of BankAmerica Corp.

Until about two years ago, syndicating a large corporate bank loan meant distributing a lengthy offering document, often running more than 200 pages, to 50 to 100 banks. It was, Rushmore recalled, a nightmarish, inefficient process that involved waves of overnight mail, constant faxing and armies of messengers.

Today, much of that process is handled over the Internet on bank Web sites that other banks tap into to read and download the offering document, ask questions and exchange views. Rushmore estimates that the Internet-based system trims 25 percent from the time it takes to close a deal, not just improving the ease of the transaction but also saving an immense amount of hours of work.

About a year ago Booz Allen & Hamilton began using the Internet to bill several federal agencies that are its clients. Booz Allen estimates that it has saved $150,000 a year by eliminating the paper handling on its $10 million in monthly billings to the government. The greater speed and efficiency of the electronic billing also means that the consulting firm is being paid 30 percent, or six days, faster than before.

"Getting that money into the bank much more quickly is probably the biggest benefit," said Mark Arnsberger, an assistant controller for Booz Allen & Hamilton.

The rapid spread of Internet-based computing, experts say, promises to compress the time it takes for any new technology to enhance economic welfare in general. The classic study of the phenomenon, *The Dynamo and the Computer: An Historical Perspective on the Modern Productivity Paradox*, by Paul David, an economic historian at Stanford University, was published in 1990.

The electric motor, David noted, was introduced in the early 1880s but did not generate discernible productivity gains until the 1920s. It took that long, he wrote, not only for the technology to be widely distributed but also for businesses to reorganize work around the industrial productionline, the efficiency breakthrough of its day.

"The process takes longer than people think, but I still believe that we will get a revival of productivity growth led by the spread of computing," David said.

His is a misplaced faith, according to the dwindling band of techno-pessimists whose own beliefs remain unshaken. Sure, they concede, there has been surprisingly strong productivity growth for the last three years. Could this represent a break in the trend? Possibly, they grudgingly admit, but only a tiny shift at best, they insist.

The real problem, they explain, lies in the composition of the nation's vast service economy. More than half of all white-collar workers are what they term "knowledge workers"—managers, executives and professionals like doctors, lawyers, teachers, even economists.

"The work they do does not lend itself to technology-driven improvements in productivity, and any gains are really difficult to eke out and are glacial," said Stephen Roach, chief economist at Morgan Stanley Dean Witter. "Paul

David's electrical motor has nothing to do with the knowledge-intensive process of work in a service economy."

The real technology cynic at the Fed meeting on Thursday will be Paul Strassmann, a former chief information officer of Xerox and the Pentagon. Strassmann, author of *The Squandered Computer*, published in 1997, believes that corporate America's spending spree on information technology amounts to an "economic arms race," fueled by misguided management theories.

The recent improvement in productivity, according to Strassmann, is mainly attributable to the lower cost of capital because of low interest rates. His summary view, though at odds with those of technology optimists like Brynjolfsson of MIT, may also be received warmly by the Fed.

"The explanation for the productivity improvement is interest rates, not information technology," Strassmann said. "The hero here is not Bill Gates. It's Alan Greenspan."

Yet even Strassmann finds the technology undeniably useful, if not a productivity elixir. When asked a detailed question, he replied, "Just look it up on my Web site. It's a lot more efficient that way."

The New York Times, April 14, 1999
http://www.nytimes.com/library/tech/99/04/biztech/articles/14tech.html

CRITICAL THINKING QUESTIONS

1. Based upon what you have read in this article, why do you think technology is essential to the production and distribution of goods and services?
2. Do you believe most industries could function without technology today? Explain your response.
3. Where do you think the emphasis should be placed when determining how technology shapes our economy?

STORY-SPECIFIC QUESTIONS

1. Explain why economists now view technology as a benefit to economic growth and productivity.
2. What are examples of how the Internet and related technology has improved efficiency in business transactions?
3. Explain why Paul Strassman disagrees with the viewpoint that technology has improved productivity.

SHORT APPLICATION ASSIGNMENTS

1. In teams or individually, answer the story-specific questions; keep your answers to 25–75 words for each question.

2. In teams of three to five persons each, or as a whole class, discuss your responses to the critical thinking questions.
3. Prepare a one-page memo report (200–250 words) to your instructor in which you summarize this article. You will find a model one-page report on the Web site (nytimes.swcollege.com).
4. Write an executive summary (200–250 words). As an administrative assistant to a busy executive, you are expected to summarize selected articles and present important points. You will find a model executive summary on the Web site.
5. Summarize this article (100–125 words) for your company's newsletter. You will find a model newsletter on the Web site.

BUILDING RESEARCH SKILLS

1. Individually or in teams, research the communication and networking technology trends over the last 25 years. Your instructor may ask you to submit a three- to five-page summary, post a Web page or report your results in a five-minute presentation, along with a letter of transmittal explaining your summary.
2. Using at least three other references (e.g., books, research-journal articles, newspaper or magazine stories or credible Web sites), write an 800- to 1,000-word essay that addresses two of the critical thinking questions offered earlier. Assume that your essay will be used as an internal reference for a government's policy guidelines.
3. Using at least three other references (e.g., books, research-journal articles, newspaper or magazine stories or credible Web sites), post an 800- to 1,000-word Web page that addresses at least two of the earlier critical thinking questions. Assume that your page will be posted in the policy section of a government's intranet.

Debate on Internet Taxes Takes Political Turn

By Jeri Clausing

Politics and business appear headed for a clash when an elite group of high-technology and government leaders appointed by Congress to draft sales tax policies for the Internet meets in New York this week.

At their first meeting this summer, in Williamsburg, Virginia, most in the group, the 19-member Advisory Commission on Electronic Commerce, seemed to agree that Internet sales should be subject to the same taxes levied on sales in the physical world. The key question, they said, was how to devise a more uniform tax rate or a system that would make it easy for companies, whether big or small, to collect the taxes levied by more than 30,000 state and local jurisdictions.

But the panel's chairman, Governor James Gilmore of Virginia, a Republican with an aggressive antitax agenda, says he is not convinced Internet sales should be taxed.

That view has triggered suspicions among some business members that their colleagues from the political arena may be inclined to stifle any solution that could be construed as a new tax levy.

An aide to a high-technology representative on the commission, who asked not to be identified, said a workable solution was being circulated that called for businesses to collect sales taxes on Internet commerce if state and local governments agree to adopt a single tax rate for each state or commit to new technologies in the form of free, easy-to-use software to enable companies to calculate any tax rate.

"Most of the commission members, plain as day, can see a deal right in front of them," said the aide. "But the commission staff is pushing it away."

Gilmore denies trying to stifle debate on any proposal and says he simply wants to insure that all sides get a fair hearing, including whether sales taxes even have a place on the Internet.

"There are some folks who are in the commission and around the commission who do not believe that this is the issue," Gilmore said. "They assume already that taxes should apply to the Internet and electronic commerce, and they do not believe any discussion ought to be held about that."

The commission was created last year as part of federal legislation imposing a three-year moratorium on any new state or local taxes on Internet access or sales.

Composed of eight business representatives, eight politicians from state and local governments and three members of the Clinton administration, the panel was supposed to begin work in December. But that was delayed when groups representing state, county and city governments—concerned about losing the tax revenues that pay for many crucial operations—complained that congressional leaders had appointed too many business representatives.

Adjustments were made, and those same state and local groups expressed pleasant surprise when many of the key business members sided with them at the commission's first meeting.

C. Michael Armstrong, chairman and chief executive of AT&T; Theodore Waitt, chairman and chief executive of Gateway, and David Pottruck, president of Charles Schwab, voiced support for taxing Internet commerce as long as a new, simpler and equitable system could be devised.

Although state and local governments the last four decades have been unable to agree on a simple way to collect sales taxes from mail-order companies, some are optimistic that the threat of losing huge revenue opportunities from taxes on Internet sales might inspire a solution.

"We recognize that the present system is a mess and needs to be addressed through simplicity and uniformity," said Neal Osten, director of the National Conference of State Legislatures' Commerce and Communications Committee. "We need to make it easier for companies to comply."

The commission also contains strong tax opponents, however, like Grover Norquist, president of Americans for Tax Reform, who has proposed using the insurgence of the Internet as an opportunity to get rid of sales taxes.

Whether or not the commission can reach a consensus and draft a comprehensive proposal for Congress by next year, Gilmore says that at least it can clearly define the issues for Congress. In addition to sales tax, the group is expected to study international tax issues on the Internet and taxes on Internet access. He said the group hoped to have a final report to lawmakers next spring.

The New York Times, September 13, 1999
http://www.nytimes.com/library/tech/99/09/biztech/articles/13pane.html

CRITICAL THINKING QUESTIONS

1. Is taxing one's use of the Internet fair or necessary? Explain why.
2. Should the government intervene in private enterprise to the extent that taxing serves as a means of generating revenue? Why, or why not?
3. Should sales from mail order catalog sales be subject to state and local taxes? Why, or why not?

STORY-SPECIFIC QUESTIONS

1. Why was the Advisory Committee on Electronic Commerce established?
2. Explain James Gilmore's opposition to a uniform taxing policy.
3. What position was taken by business on the Internet sales tax?

SHORT APPLICATION ASSIGNMENTS

1. In teams or individually, answer the story-specific questions; keep your answers to 25–75 words for each question.
2. In teams of three to five persons each, or as a whole class, discuss your responses to the critical thinking questions.
3. Prepare a one-page memo report (200–250 words) to your instructor in which you summarize this article. You will find a model one-page report on the Web site (nytimes.swcollege.com).
4. Write an executive summary (200–250 words). As an administrative assistant to a busy executive, you are expected to summarize selected articles and present important points. You will find a model executive summary on the Web site.
5. Summarize this article (100–125 words) for your company's newsletter. You will find a model newsletter on the Web site.
6. Participate in a panel discussion on the pros and cons of conducting business on the Internet.

BUILDING RESEARCH SKILLS

1. Individually or in teams, research how 10 corporations or major industries utilize the Internet to conduct business. What are their opinions regarding the proposal to tax Internet users? Your instructor may ask you to submit a three- to five-page summary, post a Web page or report your results in a five-minute presentation, along with a letter of transmittal explaining your essay.
2. Individually or in teams, review three of the proposals submitted to the Advisory Committee on Electronic Commerce (http://www.ecommercecommission.org/proposal.htm). Your instructor may ask you to submit a three- to five-page summary, post a Web page or report your results in a five-minute presentation, along with a letter of transmittal explaining your essay.
3. Individually or in teams, review the web sites of the Advisory Commission on Electronic Commerce (http://www.ecommercecommission.org/), Information Technology Association of America (http://www.itaa.org/) and Internet Tax Fairness Coalition (http://www.nettaxfairness.org/). Who sponsors these pages? What is their position on Internet taxation? Your instructor may ask you to submit a three- to five-page summary, post a Web page or report your results in a five-minute presentation, along with a letter of transmittal explaining your essay.
4. Using at least three other references (e.g., books, research-journal articles, newspaper or magazine stories or credible Web sites), write an 800- to 1,000-word essay that addresses two of the critical thinking questions offered earlier. Assume that your essay will be used as an internal reference for a government's policy guidelines.
5. Using at least three other references (e.g., books, research-journal articles, newspaper or magazine stories or credible Web sites), post an 800- to 1,000-word Web page that addresses at least two of the earlier critical thinking questions. Assume that your page will be posted in the policy section of a government's intranet.

Internet Tax Panel Faces Thorny Issues

By Jeri Clausing

A panel of technology and government leaders appointed to study Internet tax issues opened its second meeting on Tuesday with a reminder from House Republican leaders that its job is to decide whether or not to tax Internet transactions, not how to tax them.

The letter, signed by House Majority Leader Dick Armey and 34 colleagues, came as the members of the 19-member Advisory Commission on Electronic Commerce were trying to line up support behind competing proposals that will shape their report to Congress.

"We recognize the challenge you face, as members of this national commission, in trying to tackle some very important issues regarding the future of e-commerce," the letter said. " . . . We are concerned, however, about the fact that most of the news reports from the first commission meeting seemed to focus on how to tax the Internet, rather than whether to tax the Internet."

The Congressional leaders went on to remind the commission that "only Congress can authorize one state to compel sellers in another state to collect Internet taxes. This idea is not a popular one in Congress or among the American people. You should also know that there are many members that will oppose any new taxes on the Internet."

While copies of that letter were being circulated at the meeting, the Information Technology Association of America released the results of a Gallup poll showing that 73 percent of active Internet users oppose an Internet sales tax. It also showed that more than a third of registered voters who are active Internet users would be less likely to vote for a political candidate who supports taxes on Internet sales.

The letter and study are just the latest indications of how politically thorny the commission's task is, and why such odd alliances are in the works between business leaders, state and local politicians and anti-tax advocates charged with sifting through the complex issues.

The commission was appointed by Congress last year to recommend tax policy for the Internet age. Although it is charged with studying a variety of issues, from taxes on telecommunications and Internet access to international taxes, the key question it has been asked to decide is whether and how state and local sales taxes should be applied to Internet transactions.

Although representatives of state and local governments—concerned that a permanent moratorium on Internet sales taxes would make it impossible for them to fund basic public services—have wrangled the support of the some of the business representatives on the panel, the alliances are anything but clear.

Virginia Governor James Gilmore, the panel's chairman and a conservative Republican, says he is not sure sales taxes should be applied to electronic commerce.

And Dean Andal, chairman of California's tax administration board, will propose a plan on Wednesday that would codify into law the system followed by most mail-order businesses. State and local governments have complained for years that this system, under which companies only collect taxes from customers in states where they have a substantial physical presence, already deprives them of billions of dollars in revenues.

But Andal insists that the growth of electronic commerce is more than making up for any lost revenue from sales taxes. He says California, which has some of the most Internet-friendly laws in the country, had $2 billion in unexpected sales tax revenue last year.

"There no question that some tax goes uncollected. The real question is whether it's significant enough to upset interstate commerce" with a complex tax system, he said.

And while business leaders would be expected to fall in line behind Andal's proposal, some are working with representatives of state and local governments on a plan that would give states a guarantee that companies will begin collecting and paying sales taxes if the states simplify their taxation structure. There are now more than 30,000 tax jurisdictions with varying tax rates and rules in the country.

The panel is expected to begin discussing its various options on Wednesday, but no final recommendations are expected until spring.

Commission member Grover Norquist, president of Americans for Tax Reform, plans to ask his colleagues to support three resolutions. One would voice support for the Clinton Administration's opposition to new Internet tariffs. The others would abolish the 3 percent federal tax on telecommunications services, along with all Internet access taxes and fees.

Norquist said his talks with the other panel members indicate he has a "super majority," but he wants a vote to confirm that.

He offered the resolutions after the commission heard Tuesday from several business representatives who urged the panel to recommend that Congress repeal taxes on telephone service, including the 3 percent federal excise tax.

That tax, Norquist said, "was put in place to fund the Spanish-American War. Although I attended public school, I understand that war's over."

CyberTimes, The New York Times on the Web, September 15, 1999
http://www.nytimes.com/library/tech/99/09/cyber/articles/15tax.html

CRITICAL THINKING QUESTIONS

1. How, and under what circumstances, should taxes be applied to Internet activities?
2. Should certain Internet transactions carry more weight than others when one considers taxing Internet activity? Explain.

3. Should Internet users outside of the United States have to pay taxes on products bought from Web sites in the United States? Why, or why not?

STORY-SPECIFIC QUESTIONS

1. What, according to this article, is the biggest task of the Advisory Commission?
2. Summarize the results of the Gallup Poll provided by Information Technology Association of America.
3. What sales tax revenue problems are "experienced" by mail-order businesses?

SHORT APPLICATION ASSIGNMENTS

1. In teams or individually, answer the story-specific questions; keep your answers to 25–75 words for each question.
2. In teams of three to five persons each, or as a whole class, discuss your responses to the critical thinking questions.
3. Prepare a one-page memo report (200–250 words) to your instructor in which you summarize this article. You will find a model one-page report on the Web site (nytimes.swcollege.com).
4. Write an executive summary (200–250 words). As an administrative assistant to a busy executive, you are expected to summarize selected articles and present important points. You will find a model executive summary on the Web site.
5. Summarize this article (100–125 words) for your company's newsletter. You will find a model newsletter on the Web site.
6. Participate in a panel discussion on the pros and cons of conducting business on the Internet.

BUILDING RESEARCH SKILLS

1. Individually or in teams, research how 10 corporations or major industries utilize the Internet to conduct business. What are their opinions regarding the proposal to tax Internet users? Your instructor may ask you to submit a three- to five-page summary, post a Web page or report your results in a five-minute presentation, along with a letter of transmittal explaining your essay.
2. Individually or in teams, review three of the proposals submitted to the Advisory Committee on Electronic Commerce (http://www.ecommercecommission.org/ proposal.htm). Your instructor may ask you to submit a three- to five-page summary, post a Web page or report your results in a five-minute presentation, along with a letter of transmittal explaining your essay.
3. Individually or in teams, review the web sites of the Advisory Commission on Electronic Commerce (http://www.ecommercecommission.org/), Information Technology Association of America (http://www.itaa.org/) and Internet Tax Fairness Coalition (http://www.nettaxfairness.org/). Who sponsors these pages? What is their position on Internet taxation? Your instructor may ask you to submit a three- to five-page

summary, post a Web page or report your results in a five-minute presentation, along with a letter of transmittal explaining your essay.

4. Using at least three other references (e.g., books, research-journal articles, newspaper or magazine stories or credible Web sites), write an 800- to 1,000-word essay that addresses two of the critical thinking questions offered earlier. Assume that your essay will be used as an internal reference for a government's policy guidelines.

5. Using at least three other references (e.g., books, research-journal articles, newspaper or magazine stories or credible Web sites), post an 800- to 1,000-word Web page that addresses at least two of the earlier critical thinking questions. Assume that your page will be posted in the policy section of a government's intranet.